Words of Life

The Bible Day by Day
January–April 2010

HODDER &
STOUGHTON

First published in Great Britain in 2009 by Hodder & Stoughton
An Hachette Livre UK company

1

A CIP catalogue record for this title is available from the British Library

ISBN 978 0 340 99540 2

Typeset in Minion by Avon DataSet Ltd, Bidford on Avon, Warwickshire

Printed and bound in Great Britain
by Clays Ltd, St Ives plc

Hodder & Stoughton policy is to use papers that are natural, renewable
and recyclable products and made from wood grown in sustainable forests.
The logging and manufacturing processes are expected to conform to the
environmental regulations of the country of origin.

Hodder & Stoughton Ltd
338 Euston Road
London NW1 3BH

www.hodderfaith.com

Contents

Sundays

Most of the Sunday readings focus on the poetry of the psalms.

From the writer of *Words of Life*

In this edition of *Words of Life*, the drama of the Word comes alive in eight acts. The first and final acts come from the Gospel of Mark. The first act – four chapters from Mark – starts with Jesus at the Jordan River and in the wilderness. The final act places us with the disciples and Jesus near the source of the Jordan in the area of Mount Hermon, where we hear Peter's great confession, 'You are the Christ!'

Between the opening and closing acts of Mark we view a drama from the sometimes obscure Old Testament Song of Songs and then an interlude about our journeys on foot follows. The apostle Paul's first letter to the Corinthians and guest writer Commissioner Makoto Yoshida draw us into New Testament scenes surrounding the cross of Christ.

What General Albert Orsborn said of mysteries might also be said of our next focus, paradox:

> We dwell in the midst of mysteries, and we are ourselves mysterious creatures. Our unresolved interrogatives circle the globe and fill the skies, but we go on living, though we fail in knowing. So many facts must be accepted without explanation. This is true of spiritual as well as of material things.

Tableaux vivants (living pictures) probably began in medieval liturgical dramas. They are at times still employed, bringing well-known paintings or engravings to life on stage. As we enter our *tableaux vivants*, let's pray that we will be drawn into new encounters with the Living Word.

On most Sundays we consider various psalms, source of many songs of the Church and quoted more frequently than any other book by Christ and the apostles. Dietrich Bonhoeffer said that Christ is the secret of the psalms. We start with Psalm 150, a psalm of praise, and walk backwards toward the first.

Evelyn Merriam
New York, USA

Abbreviations

AB The Amplified Bible. Copyright © 1965 Zondervan.

JBP *The New Testament in Modern English*, J. B. Phillips, Geoffrey Bles, 1958.

MSG *The Message*, Eugene H. Peterson. © 1993, 1994, 1995, 1996, 2000, 2001, 2002. Used by permission of NavPress Publishing Group.

NASB New American Standard Bible. © 1995.

NKJV New King James Bible ®. Copyright © 1982 by Thomas Nelson, Inc. Used by permission. All rights reserved.

NLT New Living Translation.

SASB *The Song Book of The Salvation Army*. Copyright © 1986 The General of The Salvation Army.

TNIV Today's New International Version. Copyright © 2004 by International Bible Society. Used by permission of Hodder & Stoughton Publishers, an Hachette UK company. All rights reserved. 'TNIV' is a registered trademark of International Bible Society.

YLT *Young's Literal Translation*, Robert Young (1898) reprinted by Baker Book House, Grand Rapids, Michigan, USA.

Mark My Word

Introduction

Each August in USA Eastern Territory, the Territorial Arts Ministries Conservatory staff and students gather to develop excellence in the arts as well as personal spiritual development for the glory of God. Their *Mark My Word*,[1] focusing on Mark's Gospel, is scripted to bring Scripture to life using drama, dance, mime, choro-drama video and musical underscoring. Simple black costumes and minimal props – four black cubes, two ladders, yellow ropes, a sash and a sign pole – are a perfect fit for the briefest, most brusque of the Gospels.

Mark was the first to bring out a Gospel – possibly as early as AD 50. Matthew and Luke used some of Mark's record as source material. Through economy of words Mark gives a succinct yet compelling picture of Christ. It's as if he is the first reporter on the scene and feels the pressure of deadline. Mark writes his account for Christians in Rome. We know this in part because he sometimes explains customs and terms that a Jewish-only audience would have readily understood.

Whereas Matthew shows Christianity as the fulfilment of Judaism and Luke displays Jesus as Saviour for the world, Mark doesn't seem to have a single theme unless it's that God's Servant has arrived. Mark is a reporter of the facts as they present themselves rather than as they are tied to the past or future. He gives us specifics about Jesus the God Man. He records few parables, gives dialogue more than discourse and lists specific details of people, places, times, numbers and deeds. Some of his details help to fill in the Matthew and Luke accounts.

Mark frequently uses the word *euthys* (meaning 'without further ado') as we might expect since his mentor is impetuous Peter. We sense him tucking his equivalent of a reporter's notebook into his pocket, gathering up his robe and running ahead.

Mark details more than external facts, he gives detail of people's emotions as well. He also portrays the tenderness of Jesus. He does all this in his abrupt, concise style without the polished diction Luke or John employ. The Gospel of Mark is a living exhibition. He paints with bold, quick words as he rushes to complete the picture. The paint is still wet. But since he uses more colours from his palette, he gives us a vibrant portrait of the life of Christ.

Greater

'The beginning of the gospel about Jesus Christ, the Son of God' (v. 1).

We finished December with comments about the opening chapters of Matthew's Gospel. Now in the new year we turn to Mark's. The first verse could be its title or its theme. He says that what he records is the proclaimed good news about God's power to save us through his Son, Jesus. Mark states it is the beginning of that Gospel. That is, it gives the facts of Christ's life, death and resurrection, not what happened subsequently when the message was spread as the Church began.

The proclaimed good news is about Jesus, the Greek version of the Hebrew *Jehoshua* or Joshua, meaning 'Yahweh is salvation'. It is about the Christ, the Greek version of the Hebrew *Masah* or Messiah meaning 'the Anointed One'. It is about the Son of God. Mark uses this title to underscore Jesus' divinity and Jesus' relationship with God the Father whom he obeys.

In his introduction Mark highlights three events that prepared Jesus for his mission. Matthew 3–4 included them as well: John the Baptist's ministry as forerunner, Jesus' baptism and his desert temptation. Mark ties his record with the Old Testament in verses 2 and 3. Aside from when quoting Jesus, this is Mark's only reference from the Old Testament. Verse 2 refers to preparation of the way which Mark takes to be the way for the Messiah. God would send John ahead of Jesus to urge Israel to get ready for their Messiah.

Verses 4 to 8 briefly explain how John carried out his mission of preparation. Mark summarises John's proclamation, then points to its purpose, the declaration of the imminent arrival of the 'coming one' and his greater baptism. John declares the coming one as more powerful and more worthy.

Christ's baptism would not be one with merely an outward sign of water, but one with the incomparable, revitalising Holy Spirit. Christ still offers such a baptism to any who come to him in repentance and faith.

To pray:

'Give us faith, O Lord, we pray; faith for greater things.'

Albert Orsborn (SASB 769)

River and Desert Places

'The moment he came out of the water, he saw the sky split open and God's Spirit, looking like a dove, come down on him. Along with the Spirit, a voice: "You are my Son, chosen and marked by my love, pride of my life" ' (vv. 10, 11, MSG).

Even in the first verses of Mark's Gospel we sense his abrupt style. Perhaps it reflects the urgency of his message. Or since it is believed that Peter, whom Mark mentions early in the Gospel, was one of Mark's principal sources, perhaps more than a trace of the bold disciple's mode influences the text.

In contrast with other people who come to John from the regions of Judea and Jerusalem, Jesus comes to the desert region from an obscure northern village, Nazareth in Galilee. Also in contrast with others who came to John, Jesus does not come confessing sins. But he does submit to baptism and to John's role in God's plan for him.

Jesus makes the river an altar for his dedication to and entrance into God's mission of salvation. Later he would refer to his impending death as a baptism (10:38). Jesus may have even had his cross in mind at the Jordan River.

In verse 10 Mark uses the adverb *euthys* – immediately, straightway, at once – for the first of more than forty times in his account. The quick transition adds to the clarity of the picture and moves the account along.

As soon as Jesus emerged from the water, he saw the sky split or torn open. God broke into our human predicament. We might also think of the curtain in the temple that was torn from top to bottom at the moment of Christ's death.

In this singular moment God's Spirit descends on Jesus and he hears God's voice. Jesus has been announced by a man, then anointed by the Holy Spirit and assured and affirmed by God.

Right away the same Spirit drove Jesus into the desert. Mark's verb is stronger than Luke's or Matthew's 'led' (v. 12). God was on the offensive, not avoiding evil, but encountering it head on. Satan assails Jesus in the desert where the Spirit had taken him. The 'Spirit' and the 'desert' recur in Mark's first thirteen verses. In the desert place Jesus triumphs. He still does if we let him.

On Earth as it is in Heaven

'Hallelujah! For our Lord God Almighty reigns' (Revelation 19:6).

Psalm 150, possibly written as a final doxology to the book of Psalms, is a beautiful song of praise and a fitting start for the Sundays of our new year. The psalmist prescribes the fundamental where, why, how and who of praise.

The writer enjoins us to praise God in his sanctuary and in his heaven. We think of what Jesus prayed: 'Your kingdom come, your will be done on earth as it is in heaven' (Matthew 6:10). Although there can be many other times and places, on this Lord's Day we take time to praise God with other believers in his house. May our prayers, songs, gifts, music and other expressions be heartfelt and a reflection of the worship in heaven.

In verse 2 the psalmist simply tells us to praise God for what he does and who he is. Not only did our Creator fashion our world, but he cares about it and maintains it. God personally intervened in human history to offer redemption. God accomplishes his purposes, sometimes through extraordinary means and often through his people.

God can do this and more because of who he is. When we praise him for his greatness, in what ways do we consider it? To start, we can think about God's vast creativity, God's absolute otherness, unsurpassed power, uniqueness, glory, righteousness, wisdom, holiness, intimacy with humanity and pure love.

How can we begin to praise God? Humankind alone of all creation has choices of expression. In the context of the times, the psalmist proposes wind and string instrumental music, percussion and dance and human voice.

We are all involved in this masterpiece of praise. Not just those who can keep beat in time, pluck or blow a tune, or move rhythmically, but every voice should offer God praise. Revelation 4:11 describes a unison declaration of praise: 'You are worthy, our Lord and God, to receive glory and honour and power, for you created all things, and by your will they were created and have their being.' Amen.

To ponder:

Praise God in all places, for all things, by all means.

It's Time

' "The time has come," he said. "The kingdom of God is near.
Repent and believe the good news!" ' (v. 15).

Jesus' ministry in Galilee began after John was imprisoned – literally after John was 'handed over or delivered up'. Mark uses the same verb when he speaks of Jesus' betrayal by Judas (3:19). Mark may have connected the two men's unwarranted experiences in retrospect as key in the unfolding purposes of God.

Jesus comes. He comes to Galilee. He comes speaking publicly. He comes speaking of good news. He comes speaking of good news of God's kingdom. Jesus comes. He comes to our town. He comes relaying good news of God's kingdom. There's hope and life in the words Jesus speaks.

What does Jesus say? His message is fourfold. First he says that it's time! At long last the time is ripe. The word Mark uses for time is not *chronos* (a date on the calendar) but *kairos* (the opportune time). God's appointed time for the long-awaited Messiah is fulfilled. It could have been Israel's moment of glory.

Second, he says God's reign has arrived. As a result, the third and fourth parts of his message are charges to turn from trusting anything else and to commit to the core of the good news, God's Son incarnate. This is the only way into God's kingdom. The kingdom has come spiritually and will yet come more completely one day when God's rule will be recognised openly.

Salvation Army songwriter Joy Webb writes of blessings of accepting God's kingdom personally:

> When Jesus comes to you, he'll bring gladness,
> When Jesus comes to you, he'll bring peace.
> The glory of his presence from care will bring release,
> When Jesus, Jesus comes to you.
>
> *Joy Webb* © The Salvation Army

To ponder:

Jesus' call makes sense to the first four people he seeks out to be his followers: Peter, Andrew, James and John. They turn to follow Christ with full allegiance. How do we respond?

Up at the Synagogue

'And they go on to Capernaum, and immediately, on the Sabbaths,
having gone into the synagogue, he was teaching' (v. 21, YLT).

Mark's narrative is up and running. Right after Jesus calls four disciples, he's off to the synagogue. Mark uses the word meaning *immediately* or *straightway* again (v. 21). He may have abbreviated events to stress big themes such as the importance and meaning of true discipleship for all believers, not just the initial twelve.

Peter, Andrew, James and John accompany Jesus to regular worship – this time in their native Capernaum. Mark may mention this as a typical Sabbath. That day Jesus has opportunity to teach at the synagogue, probably by invitation.

Mark often points out that Jesus teaches as an ongoing part of his ministry in many settings. Yet Mark seldom tells us what material Jesus covers. Does he explain the Scriptures in a vivid way? Does he speak out about social justice? Synagogues served as children's schools and small claims courts during the week and as places of worship pointing to the temple on the Sabbath. In a sense, Jesus combines the functions.

We learn that Jesus' delivery and message astound his hearers. He teaches with conviction, authority and an ability to stir hearts and minds and induce decision – quite different from what they are used to in their scribes. Who is he?

Jesus' presence and teaching provoke one man who has nothing at all in common with him to call out and identify him as Jesus, the Nazarene, the Holy One of God (v. 24). A demon knows the source of Jesus' power and authority. Jesus orders it out of the man and it obeys with a shriek.

People recognise Jesus as a unique teacher, especially when he orders unclean spirits to leave and they do just that. Soon Jesus becomes the talk of the whole Galilee region.

———

To ponder:

In what settings do I best learn? Do I encounter the Living Word in such a setting?

Epiphany

'Jesus replied, "Let us go somewhere else – to the nearby villages – so I can preach there also. That is why I have come"' (v. 38).

Right after synagogue, Jesus and the four disciples go to Peter and Andrew's house. They waste no time telling Jesus that the hostess of the home is sick with a fever. It's the Sabbath, yet Jesus heals her and she ministers to them. Others wait until evening when Sabbath is officially over to bring their sick and possessed loved ones to Jesus. It seems like the whole town turns up. Jesus heals the sick and relieves the possessed of their demons. Everyone must be tired after a full day.

No one notices that Jesus slips out early to pray in a quiet place. This is one of three times Mark portrays Jesus involved in critical prayer. They are times when he could have accomplished his mission with less cost, but through prayer he persevered in obedience to the divine plan (6:46; 14:32–42).

Peter and friends go out to hunt him down and when they discover Jesus, they tell him that people are clamouring for him – as if he should return and take advantage of popular demand. On the contrary and in part for that reason, Jesus says they need to move on to share the good news in other places.

In the church calendar, today is Epiphany. The term means 'first appearance', a debut of sorts. On this day some parts of the Church celebrate the coming of the Magi to see Jesus while other parts celebrate Jesus' baptism. The visit of the Magi signifies Christ's appearance for the Gentiles while Jesus' baptism signifies the expression of his humanity as the Son of God at the outset of his mission. Before Christmas was introduced, in the early Church, Epiphany celebrated both Jesus' birth *and* baptism.

After Capernaum, Jesus visits towns throughout Galilee, probably for several weeks. No doubt for each place and person it was a memorable 'epiphany', eternally significant for those who embraced his good news.

———

To ponder:

What have Christ's 'epiphanies' in my life been? Let's ask the Lord to help us to prepare the way for his 'epiphany' in another's life.

Hopeful Becomes Joyful

'If we confess our sins, he is faithful and just and will forgive us our sins and purify us from all unrighteousness' (1 John 1:9).

What gives a person hope? The leper must be hopeful when he approaches Jesus for healing. But what is his basis for hope? The Old Testament warned people to avoid lepers and only recorded two healings of leprosy – Miriam's and Naaman's. Anyone deemed 'unclean' was to avoid society and was even segregated in worship.

Yet the man neither presumes nor doubts the possibility of healing as he approaches Jesus. We wonder if he fears rejection. Jesus allays the man's fears and confirms his hope. With deep pity Jesus touches the untouchable and heals the incurable. Then he underscores his action with his authority: 'I am willing,' he says. 'Be clean' (v. 41). Christ's dual declaration and deed produce a complete demonstrable cure *immediately*.

And *right away* Jesus sends the man off with a stern warning not to talk about his healing, but in compliance with Mosaic law to go to the priest for verification and to offer prescribed sacrifices as further proof. Such a testimony could be incriminating evidence if the priest rejected the healer of the former leper.

Jesus forbids spreading the word to avoid unnecessary antagonism toward the gospel or attraction of favour-seeking crowds. But the man can't contain his joy and freely tells his story. Consequently Jesus' open ministry in towns in Galilee is disrupted. His act of compassion is costly to his mission. He withdraws to remote areas. Still the people come to him from everywhere.

Leprosy is perverse. Besides eroding tissue and producing ulcers, as it progresses it deadens nerves and prevents both pleasurable and painful feeling. Although we don't desire pain, it can be a gift when it alerts us to and prevents us from further injury. Leprosy overrides pain's warnings and deadens sensitivity to hot, cold, heavy or sharp objects – allowing injury.

Sin can deaden our spiritual sensitivities and allow us to become mortally wounded. But there is hope in Christ. As our key verse declares, God is willing to effect forgiveness for all confessed sin and to cleanse our hearts. So we, like the unnamed patient, can continue to live hopefully and joyfully.

'We Never Have Done it Like This Before'

'This amazed everyone and they praised God, saying, "We have never seen anything like this!"' (v. 12).

Mark presses fast-forward to the next incident he wants to describe. Jesus is back in Capernaum, probably at Peter's house. No social posting announces that he is 'at home and receiving visitors'. But word spreads and invited or not, *immediately* people crowd into the house. Jesus teaches the word in an everyday way.

Meanwhile there are too many people and no disabled entrance for four latecomers with a paralysed friend. They aren't deterred. Like rushing water meeting resistance, they and their charge flow up and over the obstacle to reach their goal. Jesus is impressed by the faith of the five and goes beyond their obvious expectations and forgives the paralytic.

The scribes with prime seats in the standing-room-only crowd are shocked. What a nerve of Jesus to offer forgiveness! Who does he think he is – God? Instantly Jesus knows their objections and counters them with a question that bewilders them: which is easier, to forgive or heal? Neither.

Yet when Jesus does both, the harder first, and the man walks away in plain sight a restored person, it refutes the scribes' protests and amazes all. In this case, physical healing validates spiritual pardon. Luke 5:16 says that all marvel at the strange things or paradoxes of that day. In Mark they give God glory (v. 12).

Surprising events continue as Jesus walks along the lakeside, notices and calls a publican from his toll booth to be his follower. Instead of collecting for the king, Matthew would collect human treasure for the King. Jesus' call to Matthew seems sudden, but he is ready to respond *at once* and not miss his opportunity.

This time it's the Pharisees who cluck about Jesus. Why does he associate with sinners? They mean the common, untaught, less observant Jews instead of righteous separatists such as themselves. Jesus knows their hearts and counters that he has not come to call the 'righteous', but sinners.

––––––––––

To ponder:

Would anyone wonder about my associations for Jesus' sake?

Not in a Museum

'No-one sews a patch of unshrunk cloth on an old garment. If he does, the new piece will pull away from the old, making the tear worse' (v. 21).

The Pharisees support fasting to keep religious custom. John's disciples may have fasted out of sorrow because John was in prison or had been martyred. Jesus says there would be time for his disciples to fast in grief later. This allusion to death is Mark's first suggestion of the crucifixion.

Jesus neither opposes fasting nor commands it, but teaches that it should spring from right motives (Matthew 6:16–18). Yet Jesus goes beyond the question of fasting to the issue of God doing a new thing. Jesus' vibrant presence on earth fulfilled what the old static forms had basically been preparation for.

His short parables about cloth and wine apply more widely than to the practice of fasting. Jesus isn't advising against repair of our possessions or care for old objects. He isn't denying the value of tradition or respect for tested faith in God and his word. In another place Jesus reminds us, 'Therefore every teacher of the law who has been instructed about the kingdom of heaven is like the owner of a house who brings out of his storeroom new treasures as well as old' (Matthew 13:52).

But his gospel in its newness and fullness isn't just a patch for a worn-out system of rigid, human rules and forms. Likewise, Jesus says old leather bottles can't handle new wine, which continues to expand as it completes its maturing process and so will crack the inflexible dried-up leather, seep out and be wasted!

It would take open minds and new thinking to embrace his mission and release fearful dependence on old customs while holding to God's changeless truth. The good news is neither a novelty fad nor another option among many to keep handy 'in case'. It's God doing a timeless thing in a fresh innovative way.

If authentic Christianity seems revolutionary in today's world, imagine how radical it seemed two thousand years ago! We preserve and appreciate heritage and tradition, but we can't live in a museum. We can live vibrantly when encountering the world directed by the One who is eternally present and contemporary: our Saviour, the I AM.

Epiphany Season

'Our God comes and will not be silent' (Psalm 50:3).

Psalm 149 calls us to worship. The psalmist praises God for salvation and vindication. He calls us to sing a new song. Perhaps that's another way of saying we should keep our thanks up to date. We're grateful for past blessings, but let's ask the Lord to keep us alert to the joys and consideration he sends today as well.

Although some observe Epiphany as a single day, 6 January, many church traditions extend Epiphany as a season running up to the start of Lent. Perhaps we will have a season of epiphanies of grace.

We're told to sing 'his praise in the assembly of the saints' (v. 1). In reflection on Messianic Psalm 22, the author of Hebrews reports Jesus saying: 'I will declare your name to my brothers; in the presence of the congregation I will sing your praises' (Hebrews 2:12). If Jesus did that, how much more should we?

Promise

He comes . . . in the thundering tumble of wind
down a greening hill
when all the world is wrapped in him.
He comes in a ballerina dance
of chartreuse and rosy silk –
virginal visage of beauty
lingering on the mind, promising
something you cannot forget.
He comes to the wintering ground –
ravished, silent, spent –
and wakens it to joy.
In everything he whispers, thunders,
comfort, weeps, and laughs.
'Our God comes and will not be silent.'
Marlene Chase[2]

11

Scrutinising the Lord

*'Then Jesus asked them, "Which is lawful on the Sabbath: to do good
or to do evil, to save life or to kill?" But they remained silent' (v. 4).*

He positions himself in an advantageous corner to survey the college's
coffee bar. Nothing misses his scrutiny. No one gets away with breaking his rules. His policing role gives him a sense of control. He only makes
exceptions to curry favour. Tension reigns. Students visit this coffee bar
only as a last resort.

Religious leaders continue to layer on their criticism of Christ. They
object to his right to forgive sin, his association with outsiders and his
disciples' lack of fasting. Like the coffee-bar manager who finds fault
rather than serves, the Pharisees keep watch and challenge Jesus, this time
over Sabbath-keeping. Mark's account, like Matthew's, couples objections
over eating grain in the field with that of healing a man in the synagogue,
both on the Sabbath.

The law allows people who pass by ripe fruit or grain to snack along the
way. The disciples aren't harvesting grain for future meals or stealing
someone's livelihood. The complaint is that they dare do it on the Sabbath
(as if hunger takes a holiday).

Jesus makes it clear that God made the Sabbath to benefit humankind,
not burden it with regulations. Therefore, the Son of Man is master even
of this set-apart day. The next incident illustrates his position further.

Some stare at a man with a withered hand – not out of concern for him,
but to see what Jesus will do in the synagogue on the Sabbath. Jesus meets
the challenge and clearly shows that it's more than a matter of Sabbath
observance. It's a question of doing good rather than harm in keeping with
the Sabbath principle of restoration.

Jesus is angry and distressed with the religious leaders. He grieves at
their obstinacy and what it's doing to them. Without visibly doing anything
that could be called work Jesus gives the man an instruction. He obeys and
his hand is healed.

The Pharisees take umbrage at Jesus' challenge to their authority. Even
though it is the Sabbath, in their rage they *immediately* conspire to destroy
Jesus. In verse 6, Mark explicitly refers for the first time to the sobering
destiny of Jesus' mission, his death.

Congestion Pricing

'Jesus withdrew with his disciples to the lake, and a large crowd from Galilee followed' (v. 7).

Mark tells us of eleven times when Jesus withdraws. He retreats for rest, to teach his disciples in private, to evade his enemies or to pray. This time he withdraws from the usual public places not in fear of opposition or rejection, but because it isn't yet time for the final conflict. The agitated leaders could instigate it prematurely. The open lakeside is a safer place.

Even at the shore a horde from the region and beyond follows him. No one is assigned to crowd control. There are no announcements about waiting for off-peak hours or giving priority seating to the disabled or elderly. But Mark gives a detail that someone such as Peter the fisherman could have remembered. Jesus takes the precaution of asking his disciples to prepare a small boat for him in case those frantic to touch him for healing create a chaotic rush.

We take many precautions to avoid sickness. Today, when we succumb in spite of our best efforts, we have access to medicine, doctors and therapy. The people besieging Jesus weren't as fortunate and were desperate for healing just to be able to function, to live. What did it cost Jesus to be swarmed by germs of infectious diseases, not to speak of the shrieking of demons?

Little do those people realise that *Yahweh Rophe* (meaning 'the Lord heals, binds up, mends, cures') is among them. Healing their physical maladies anticipates his greater healing of souls. On the cross, Jesus bore the consequences of our sin. He carried our souls' infirmities and sufferings. He took the whole world's sin-plagues and their ravaging symptoms on himself (Isaiah 53:4).

Christ rebukes the demons' premature announcement of his arrival as Messiah. Until Jesus could explain the true nature of the Messiah, the demons' pronouncement could ruin his mission. The popular conquering hero image could start an uprising.

———

To ponder:

How do we expect to see Christ in our world?

In Common

'Whoever does God's will is my brother and sister and mother' (v. 35).

Out of the crowds by the lake, Jesus summons some to go up the mountain with him. Then he selects a dozen for special work. We don't know why there are twelve, possibly to correspond with the twelve tribes of Israel, but they are not called a 'new Israel'. They will be the nub of a new community, the Church. Although they are selected for a mission, it isn't time for that yet. They need more time with Jesus. Of the twelve only Judas is not from Galilee.

At this point Mark skips over the Sermon on the Mount that Matthew and Luke relate and takes Jesus to 'the house' (probably Peter's). Once again it's a full house (as it had been in 1:32 and 2:2). Mark adds that Jesus and his disciples don't even have time to eat.

In verses 22 to 29 Jesus faces and refutes the religious teachers who keep accusing him of being demon-possessed. This is sandwiched between Jesus' family trying to get him out of the crowds and into their care because he seems fanatical or imbalanced. Mark notes a parallel between the charges against Jesus by family (v. 21) and by religious leaders (v. 30) yet Mark distinguishes between them too.

Jesus' mother and brothers send in the message that they want a word. The crowd between them keeps his would-be rescuers at bay. They go home without him. But their visit prompts Jesus to ask a rhetorical question – who makes up my family? He looks around at those encircling him and says that his followers are family. He isn't renouncing family ties but indicating that his family is broader than a natural family. His spiritual family includes anyone who does God's will.

Bible commentator William Barclay says true kinship is not solely a matter of blood relation. It lies in common experience, especially when people come through something together, common interest, common obedience to a leader and a common goal. Jesus' closest followers would be bound together through what they shared while with him, and afterwards.

To ponder:

In what ways am I intentionally bound together with other believers in God's family?

Timeless Truth

'With many similar parables Jesus spoke the word to them, as much as they could understand. He did not say anything to them without using a parable. But when he was alone with his own disciples, he explained everything'
(vv. 33, 34).

At the time it was unconventional. Teachers taught in synagogues. In Mark 2 and 3, Jesus not only heals but also teaches in a house and outdoors by the lake. He asks for a boat to be ready in case the crowd swells (3:9). Now he uses it as his platform.

Since Jesus experiences both public praise and religious resistance, he uses unusual methods. He tells stories to capture the hearers' attention, minimise arguments with religious leaders, make spiritual lessons concrete and cause people to think over the points. Jesus' parables spring spontaneously from obvious everyday prompts. He's a master of the form. He composes them as need arises, yet they carry timeless truths.

Parables are more condensed than allegories and focus on a single principle and application. Both parables and allegories 'enlighten the hearer by submitting to him a case in which he has apparently no direct concern, and upon which therefore a disinterested judgment may be elicited from him'.[3] Suddenly it dawns on the hearer that the conclusion applies to him.

The parables Mark selects to relate are from a larger collection. We know of more than thirty in the Gospels. In this chapter he includes the parable of the sower and seed, the lamp on a stand, the persistent seed and the mustard seed.

Jesus moves from declaring that the kingdom of God has come to describing the nature of that kingdom. We dwell in paradoxes that don't resolve themselves but move us toward truth. The secrets of the kingdom are open to anyone committed to knowing God, but the parables puzzle unbelievers ('those on the outside', v. 11).

To ponder:

What everyday circumstance could I use to relay eternal truth in a modern parable?

In Time

'The seed sprouts and grows, though he does not know how' (v. 27).

Several of Jesus' parables and sayings that Mark presents back to back in chapter 4 appear scattered separately in Matthew. It seems Mark telescopes them into one convenient place. Jesus continues to teach using common objects and scenarios and sometimes states what should be self-evident – a lamp belongs on a stand, not covered. Then just as quickly he makes an application. Truth is meant to be seen and witness meant to be given, not kept secret or hoarded.

Lest we think the advice of verse 24 remotely recommends a doctrine of works in the kingdom of God, in verses 26–29 Mark gives us Jesus' parable of the seed growing in secret. It is the only parable Mark alone records. Although it involves seed and growth, as did the earlier parable in the chapter, this one has a different point.

Jesus says it's an illustration of the kingdom. People are involved in spreading the message of the seed, but the mystery of germination and growth are God's work in receptive lives.

In optimum conditions, growth is certain. In less than ideal conditions, some plants surprise us. My husband and I were amazed to find delicate red columbine growing out of tall sheer cliffs along the Hudson River.

A woman visited The Salvation Army's Booth Hospital in Tokyo. A chaplain encouraged her to attend the nearby corps (church) for Sunday service. We sat together most Sundays. She spoke English because she was raised in Malaysia, where she met her Japanese husband. We became good friends and marvelled at her way with the exotic flowers she raised. Orchids were her favourites.

In time she committed her life to Christ. Her husband soon opposed her faith and forbade her attendance at Christian meetings. Friends visited their home. She read her Bible and prayed privately and was not bitter. As a widow, Mrs Mitani returned to the corps. She became a soldier (member). We corresponded from America. Happily, we met once more before she went to heaven.

We are called to sow, trust and be patient, knowing we're in partnership with God who is growing his kingdom. We have every reason to be hopeful.

Overwhelmed by Majesty

'They were terrified and asked each other, "Who is this? Even the wind and the waves obey him!"' (v. 41).

In the evening, after Jesus teaches at length from the boat, he suggests to his companions that they cross the lake, perhaps for relief from the crowd. The disciples weigh anchor without further preparation. Mark adds the detail that there were several vessels in the convoy. Some of Jesus' followers are experienced fishermen.

The gale-force winds Mark describes drive waves to break over the boat and fill it. He details that the exhausted Jesus is asleep at the stern on a leather steersman's cushion or bolster. These sound like the particulars of an eye-witness. Mark adds to what Matthew and Luke tell us the disciples say when they wake Jesus. Besides saying they are perishing, Mark tags on, 'Don't you care?', almost scolding Jesus for thoughtlessly sleeping through the storm.

Jesus rebukes the wind and speaks to the sea as well. *Immediately* the sea sinks to rest as if exhausted from its activity. The sudden calm must have been eerie. Matthew says the men marvel, Luke says they fear and marvel. Mark simply says they are terrified. Jesus questions their fear and their faith.

The disciples see a new side of Jesus. He can teach in parables, heal illness, drive out demons and now they see he can direct wind and waves. They are on a learning curve. They haven't realised all that his Messianic role means. They haven't recognised him to be Lord of nature before.

For now they're relieved that the gentle lapping of water against the boat has replaced the racket and danger of the storm. Their unease about the elements subsides, but their perplexity about their Master intensifies. His majesty overwhelms them. What could be next?

We sometimes call out to God in desperate circumstances. His answer, his relief, is palpable. But what happens after the storm when the danger is past and our stress level lessens? We remember our storms vividly and relate their details, but do we continue to marvel at God's power in delivering us? Do we still marvel at his majesty?

Invited to a Wedding?

'You are the most excellent of men and your lips have been anointed with grace, since God has blessed you for ever' (v. 2).

Weddings are both solemn and happy occasions, and can be over-whelming ventures. Although not the most popular month for weddings in the snow-covered north-eastern USA, three generations in our extended family celebrate wedding anniversaries in January.

Wedding customs vary around the world and according to social status. The bride's family is responsible for the wedding in the West, the groom's family in the East.

Some versions of the Bible title Psalm 45 as a wedding song. First it addresses a royal bridegroom, then his bride. Since its tune is named ('Lilies'), we know it was meant to be sung. It isn't like songs we hear at weddings today, especially if it was meant to be sung by the guests to the couple.

The psalm refers to Solomon – his wisdom, bearing and victories on behalf of truth and righteousness. It could be a companion piece to be read alongside Song of Songs, or even an abridged version of that book.

But it ultimately refers to the ideal Bridegroom, Christ, and can accordingly instruct us. Hebrews 1:8, 9 quotes verses 6 and 7 of the psalm in describing Christ's superior position over the angels. If we see the psalm as portraying the Lord, then the bride described symbolises the Church.

She is portrayed as prepared for the royal wedding and invited to leave her home and share the honours of marriage and a new life. 'His intent was that now, through the church, the manifold wisdom of God should be made known to the rulers and authorities in the heavenly realms' (Ephesians 3:10).

We think of the ultimate royal wedding with its marriage supper of the Lamb as depicted in Revelation. Our hearts need to be pure and victorious day by day in preparation for that magnificent celebration. The Holy Spirit uses the word and prayer to help us. We can also allow our Christian worship opportunities to focus our attention on our King and what he is preparing.

Christ My Companion

in Song of Songs

Introduction

Song of Songs – also known as Song of Solomon – is one of the Bible's five poetry books, the others being Job, Psalms, Proverbs and Ecclesiastes. Some of their contents comprise what is called wisdom literature. Song of Songs differs from most Old Testament poetry, which uses various names for God and includes references to aspects of religious worship. It does neither. Like other Hebrew poetry, Song of Songs often employs parallel ideas. These either contrast with or complete each other.

Some analyses of Song of Songs are exclusive. But it is possible to appreciate the book's value from several angles. We can read the book as literal marriage love poetry, as allegory, symbolism, illustration, drama or analogy (combining the symbolic and literal). For example, themes of love as mutual, exclusive and total apply to married love, as well as to the relationship of God and his people.

The brief book poses numerous interpretation puzzles. Throughout Jewish and Christian history it has been viewed in various ways. Of its 470 different Hebrew words, quite a few are unique to the book. Since the book is short (117 verses), consider reading it through in various versions.

Song of Songs was last commented on in *Words of Life* almost twenty years ago. I cautiously approach its difficult interpretation and application, but am determined to ferret out a sense of its intention.

What is the book's purpose? Does Song of Songs exist to teach us something about the relationship between God and his people, or to celebrate the joy of human love? Or both? Our aim is to grasp some of the book's principles that can help our walk with Christ.

> Hast thou not bid me love thee, God and King?
> All, all thine own, soul, heart and strength and mind.
> I see thy cross; there teach my heart to cling:
> O let me seek thee, and O let me find!
> *George Croly* (*SASB* [American edition] 975)

With Song

'The Song of Songs [the most excellent of them all] which is Solomon's'
(v. 1, AB).

Just as the 'holy of holies' means the most holy place in the tabernacle and Christ is called 'the King of kings', the 'song of songs' or 'ode of odes' is the superlative song.

Another unrivalled account – Ecclesiastes, 'vanity of vanities' – was also written by Solomon. It describes restlessness and meaninglessness, concluding that pursuing everything is vanity. By contrast, Song of Songs talks about finding rest and meaning. It ends in blessing because it deals with pursuing Christ.

Martin Luther called Song of Songs 'the high song' and that is its name in German, Swedish and Dutch. Solomon created more than a thousand songs (1 Kings 4:32). Song of Songs is thought to be his best. It is called a single song rather than a collection, such as the psalms are.

Song of Songs was also considered to excel the chief songs of Israel's history – such as those by Adam, Moses, Joshua, Deborah, Hannah or David. Rabbis considered Song of Songs especially excellent, superior to all the other songs.

Does the choice of song reflect its singer? The singers in Song of Songs sing candid, considerate, kind, supportive and responsive messages. The best of songs has the best of singers.

The Bible is about singing. Singing opens us to respond. It slides under invisible barriers to tie our emotions to our faith. Instrumental music has power, but wed it to meaningful lyrics and we're stirred, tuned and tied to abiding themes of assurance. Imagine how Song of Songs might affect us if set to music. We'll see that Song of Songs uses forthright language and exceptional singers.

———

To ponder:

What songs has the Holy Spirit used to speak to your spirit, to underscore spiritual anniversaries of your heart? Thank him, perhaps in song.

Drawn To Him

'Draw me! We will run after you! The king brings me into his apartments!
We will be glad and rejoice in you!' (v. 4, AB).

The prophetic word of God can simultaneously hold layers of past, present and future meaning. As with all Scripture, the Holy Spirit can speak to us individually at our point of need as we read it in the context of the Bible's whole message.

People hold various positions about the Song of Songs. Where we are in our spiritual walk influences our perspective. In our present study we could contemplate the book from any or all of our multiple roles as a modern man or woman, friend, worker, sibling, spouse, parent, trained or lay minister or church member. We could consider the main characters' viewpoints. However, we will primarily limit our treatment to the perspective of the Christian believer.

The principal characters in the drama are one woman and one man (if we assume that the king and the shepherd are the same person). A chorus advances action and poses rhetorical questions. Sometimes it is unclear who is speaking, other than it is a male or female, single or plural voice.

Commentators view the book's structure in different ways. One divides it into seven periods to correspond with the seven days of Jewish marriage celebrations. The most useful organisation may simply be: initial love, faltering love, growing love, transforming love and mature love.

In the opening verses of chapter 1 we note the drawing power of the Lord. When the Holy Spirit helps us to see God's unchangeable loveliness, holiness and character in Christ, we are drawn to him and his truth, knowing that he does not change.

Recognising him as King opens the way to seek to know him and serve him personally. Psalm 91 speaks of our dwelling in God's shelter and resting in his shadow. It's the position the woman in Song of Songs takes when she enters the king's chamber. The friends add that his followers love him uprightly, with unmixed motives. Or as Paul writes: 'love, which comes from a pure heart and a good conscience and a sincere faith' (1 Timothy 1:5). May God help us to be such followers of Christ.

With All My Heart

'Tell me, O you whom my soul loves, where you pasture your flock, where you make it lie down at noon' (v. 7, AB).

The woman discloses that she's dark-skinned because of too much work in the hot sun. Then she confesses that she was made keeper of the vineyards, but neglected her own vineyard. It is possible to be so busy working generally for the Lord that we burn out before we give attention to the specific things he gave us to do and which no one else will take up.

Perhaps it's time for us to ask the Lord to remind us of *his* assignment and tend to that first. By spending time with the Lord, the woman sees that it's important to be where he feeds his flock and provides rest. She knows her greatest need is to receive the sustenance and rest only his presence can provide, and her spirit craves this. But how can she find him?

To find the Shepherd she is advised to follow the tracks of the sheep. There are those who through the years have discovered what she is seeking – full satisfaction in the Lord alone – and she's counselled to do likewise and learn to discern what living in his presence means.

Today we have the testimony of Christians through the ages and around the globe available to us. If we take time to read about the faithful and associate with other followers of the Lord who also seek God, it will encourage our spirit. If we've been given oversight for those less mature in the faith, our gracious care for them can be a means of grace for us as well.

When an expert in the law asked Jesus what the greatest commandment was, he replied: 'Love the Lord your God with all your heart and with all your soul and with all your mind' (Matthew 22:37).

———

To pray:

> With all my heart, I want to love you, Lord,
> And live my life each day to know you more.
> All that is in me is yours completely.
> I'll serve you only with all my heart.
> *Babbie Mason*[4]

At His Table

'While the king was at his table, my perfume spread its fragrance' (v. 12).

We can read details in 1 Kings 4 about how amply King Solomon's table was supplied daily. In addition to his palace, his offerings at the temple, his retinue and his wisdom, the queen of Sheba was impressed by the food on his table (1 Kings 10:5).

Besides the king's fare, the woman in Song of Songs notes that the king himself was at the table. In the New Testament, Christ at the meal table provided the opportunity for intimate conversation, personal questions, adoration, and learning from his precepts and example, as well as refreshment.

The privilege of sitting at the table with the king implies the close relationship of an open heart. In Revelation 3:20 Christ says: 'If anyone hears my voice and opens the door, I will come in and eat with him, and he with me.' At the Last Supper, while at table with the disciples, Jesus says: 'If anyone loves me, he will obey my teaching. My Father will love him, and we will come to him and make our home with him' (John 14:23).

Coming to know the Lord in daily living signified by the common meal kindles our further dedication to him.

Our personal union with him and identification with him evokes the fragrance of praise. He prepares a table for us even while we're among our enemies (Psalm 23:5). Are we willing to join him at table? Can we say with Salvationist songwriter Keith Banks:

> I am coming to the table you've prepared for me.
> I am hungry, deeply hungry, for your company.
> As in the stillness I sit with you,
> I feel the strength of my love for you.
>
> I take my place; I seek your face;
> I come to be forgiv'n and graced.
> And one more thing I long to ask:
> Come and anoint me for my task.[5]

Banquet

'He has taken me to the banquet hall, and his banner over me is love' (v. 4).

The woman speaks of herself as a common wild flower (v. 1) – possibly a crocus, anemone, narcissus or tulip. It may be her modest response to the king's praise of her. He doesn't counter her analogy but goes further and affirms that although she may be like a humble flower, she stands out among the thorns. She testifies about her king in a reciprocal way as she says he's a tree that stands out as unique in the woods. The 'apple' tree may have been a lemon or apricot tree. Whatever type, it is tall, fruitful and its foliage provides needed shade. It is a symbol of protection, provision and delight.

When the king brings his beloved to his banquet house, a place of joy, he happily displays his love for her by raising a banner. Banners proclaim a message and draw those who agree with it.

As I turned the corner onto East 52nd Street in New York City, I wondered how easily I would find the address I was looking for among the countless buildings. I skirted a construction site and a multi-storeyed burgundy banner rippled slightly. On it I read: 'The Salvation Army's International Social Justice Centre'. I knew I'd found a place where I would meet people who work for things that matter to God.

The king's loved one in Song of Songs knows his protection, intimacy and assurance of love. This enlarges her confidence both in whose she is and who she is. Have I a similar assurance of the Lord's faithfulness and embrace of grace even in times of loss?

> I'm receiving from your table all you have for me,
> I am drawing strength, and building needed energy.
> I take your mercy, I drink your grace,
> I taste your goodness, your love embrace.
>
> I am resting at your table in tranquillity,
> I am thinking of the work you have assigned to me.
> As I remember your cross and pain,
> Master anoint me with grace again.

Keith Banks[5]

Song Season

'See! The winter is past; the rains are over and gone' (v. 11).

The woman refers to the king as a young stag (v. 9). Some suggest this may refer to the title of David's Psalm 22 because the psalm's title, *Aijeleth Hashshahar*, means the hind or deer of the dawn and thus points to the Resurrected Christ. This view may also come from the Gospel writers' connection of verses of the psalm with the words of Christ on the cross.

The woman recalls what the king's recognisable voice said. He called her through latticed windows to move with him to new vistas. There's more to our relationship with the Lord than private sweet communion, however precious it may be. Peter discovered that at Christ's transfiguration (Mark 9:5). We can't have the Lord strictly on our own terms. He calls us to follow his lead, to see him in greater situations. It is challenging, but he is eager to enable us.

Madame Guyon said of such a realisation:

Now his abiding presence is no longer a matter of place and time. In whatsoever circumstance you may be you can trust and believe in the ever-abiding presence of the Lord. Thus the believer is no longer bound or encumbered by mere inner feelings.[6]

The winter is past. The Hebrew word for winter here refers to a season during March and April which at one time predictably brought rain, sometimes mingled with fine hail. But the time of dormancy, gloom and confinement passes. Whatever trials we endure, they aren't endless. The smells, tastes, sounds and colours of spring return. In this chapter it's the budding grapevines and figs, the call of the returning migratory dove, the sparkle of spring flowers – all reasons for singing. Someone called it resurrection ground.

Perhaps those who live through the dreariest winters benefit most from the delights of spring. Songwriter John Gowans pens:

> Out of your darkness he calls you,
> Out of your doubt, your despair,
> Out of the wastes of your winter,
> Into the spring of his care.
>
> (*SASB* 378)

25

Close to His Heart

'Let them praise the name of the LORD, for his name alone is exalted; his splendour is above the earth and the heavens' (v. 13).

For most of Saturday morning the children on the outing were scattered throughout the park, playing, exploring, sharing chitchat. Near noon their teacher stood at the monument close to the park's centre and rang a bell. Whether the tone caught their attention or their growing appetites put them on alert, in no time, almost magically, they all assembled at the monument to eat sandwiches and to discover their afternoon assignment teams. They were unaware that the closer they came to their teacher, the closer they were to all of their classmates.

In some places this has been a week of prayer for Christian unity. At Advent we sometimes ask ourselves whether Christ is at the centre or the periphery of our activities. Perhaps the question isn't seasonal. When Christ is the centre, others things come together as well. People come together. *He* is the one who unifies believers.

Our psalm paints a grand picture of everything from angels to stars, sea creatures to snow, trees to birds, mountains to winds focusing praise on the Lord. With attention each can find a description in the panorama to capture our imagination and remind us to humbly appreciate the wonders of creation more often.

Psalm 148 starts with 'Praise the LORD from the heavens, praise him in the heights above' and ends closer to home by enjoining kings, nations, youth, elderly and children – all people on earth – to praise the name of the Lord who alone is worthy of all praise.

As we worship the Lord on his day, we join creation and, more significantly, all those who worship him the way Jesus described:

Yet a time is coming and has now come when the true worshippers will worship the Father in spirit and truth, for they are the kind of worshippers the Father seeks. God is spirit, and his worshippers must worship in spirit and in truth (John 4:23, 24).

It's the foundation for true Christian unity.

Outfoxed

'Catch for us the foxes, the little foxes that ruin the vineyards, our vineyards that are in bloom' (v. 15).

Soon after we moved to our present house we planted tulip bulbs and enjoyed a variegated garden bouquet the next spring. That encouraged us to work the rocky soil in a fenced patch and plant vegetables. We watched with pleasure as the plants matured. When the corn and tomatoes were ready to harvest, we came home to a ravaged garden. Squirrels had feasted indiscriminately. They'd taken bites of almost everything.

We bought trap-and-release cages and transported at least fifty creatures to county parks. In the next years we tried numerous other foils for those that remained. Although we also kept some deer and rabbits away, the squirrels were the peskiest marauders. Eventually we harvested some produce.

In further reports of what the king has said, besides his terms of endearment, the woman remembers his appeal to trap the plundering foxes. I don't know if little foxes ruin vines in the way squirrels decimate gardens, but I imagine that catching them early is important.

Life in Christ begins in sweetness and should continue to fruitfulness. Little hidden things can ruin it. Sometimes it's reviving an old habit; looking back with longing to life before the sacrifices of a life of obedience; sidestepping what we know is God's will for us; rationalising a choice; failing to deal with revealed sin immediately; worrying about the past or the future or trying to manipulate it.

An early-day Salvationist, Henry Stillwell, was a plasterer who had worked on St James's Palace in London. When he became a Salvation Army officer he found a way to deal with any temptation to return to his trade. In 1883, when he was sent to California and travelled from New York to the west coast by train, he gave away or bartered his tools along the way, thus arriving in California with some interesting Native American artefacts but without the means to practise his former trade. Brigadier Stillwell served as a pioneer officer until his death in 1905.

To ponder:

What little sins does the Lord want to address?

27

Grace Waits

'All night long on my bed I looked for the one my heart loves;
I looked for him but did not find him' (v. 1).

When the woman realises the king's absence she goes in quest of him. She is uncomfortable knowing he's not with her. In the city she seeks places where people gather. When trustworthy watchmen find her, she asks if they've seen him. She doesn't need to explain who. They point her in the right direction, but leave the discovery to her.

Do we sometimes miss a sense of the Lord's presence? Where do we turn – to counsel from trustworthy leaders and for the *koinonia* fellowship of the Church? These can be a means of grace, but the quest is ours alone.

Sometimes the Lord sees fit to delay the discovery. When Christ heard that Lazarus was ill, he waited before going to his friends. He explained to the disciples that the pause was for a purpose: 'It is for God's glory so that God's Son may be glorified through it' (John 11:4).

There are times when grace waits. 'It is impossible to have both the true life of faith and permanent lively feelings of the Lord's presence. In order to have him present in our feelings we must allow him liberty to come and go as he pleases.'[7]

When the woman finds the king, she clings to him, relaxes and rests. As earlier, he charges the friends not to wake her (v. 5).

In time the chorus breaks into exclamation at what they see. It's more than anyone dreamed. Here comes the king in full wedding attire (vv. 6–11). Some commentators analyse the details of the king's elaborate palanquin and see corresponding Old and New Testament symbols.

The bride needn't have worried about the king's absence. The bridegroom was preparing for their marriage in accordance with his responsibility. Does the Church long for the King's return? Can we imagine the triumphant marriage of the Lamb announced to John in Revelation? 'Blessed are those who are invited to the wedding supper of the Lamb!' (Revelation 19:9).

Eye of the Beholder

*'You're beautiful from head to toe, my dear love, beautiful beyond
compare, absolutely flawless' (v. 7, MSG).*

Right at the start of his declaration, the bridegroom tells his bride she's
beautiful. Earlier she was embarrassed about her appearance, which
seems unrefined to city dwellers. She told the women of Jerusalem not to
stare at her and explained that her dark complexion was from work in the
fields (1:6). Although she didn't meet her society's model of perfection, to
the king she was beautiful.

The king uses analogies from the pastoral setting, things his bride would
understand and value. He uses similes of birds, fruit, animals, spices, honey,
hills and springs. When we hear something unfamiliar in the context of what
we know, it helps us relax, appreciate and assimilate the new thought.

Some commentators have defined each metaphor in spiritual terms. For
example, having doves' eyes (v. 1) is said to signify having spiritual perception and single focus. They mention that the Holy Spirit is likened to a dove
and that true spiritual perception comes from him as he always keeps Jesus
in view.

Likewise, when the king speaks of a mountain of myrrh and hill of
frankincense (v. 6), some say this typifies Calvary and that the words at the
beginning of the verse, almost the same as the woman's in 2:17, here typify
resurrection life.

In verse 7, the bridegroom again declares the bride beautiful and adds
that she is without blemish. Few of us meet our culture's standards of
beauty, so the lavish praise of beauty in this chapter may make us
uncomfortable. Although such exquisiteness seems out of reach, in the
eyes of someone who loves us, we may be ideal.

If we view this praise as the Lord's for his followers, we see that Christ's
praise edifies, and he is glorified. By nature we are anything but lovely, but
when God cleanses and refines us, he perfects our spiritual good looks and
in Christ God sees us as flawless. Amazing grace!

To ponder:

**'I dressed you in my splendour and perfected your beauty, says the Sovereign
Lord'**

(Ezekiel 16:14, NLT)

Fruit of Paradise

'But the fruit of the Spirit is love, joy, peace, patience, kindness, goodness, faithfulness, gentleness and self-control' (Galatians 5:22, 23).

Perhaps you've heard of the Vinegar Bible. It's a rare edition printed in England in 1717 by John Baskett. Two of only seven remaining copies are in Nova Scotia, Canada, and New Hampshire, USA. The Vinegar Bible is valuable because of its errors, one of which gives it its name. It refers to the parable of the vineyard as the parable of the vinegar.

Vineyards and gardens, or orchards, appear frequently in Scripture – gardens more than fifty times and vineyards more than 100. Both appear frequently in Song of Songs, as metaphors or settings. In the Old Testament, one of the most important metaphors to describe Israel was the vine or vineyard of God (Isaiah 5:7). In Matthew 20, Jesus introduces his parable of the vineyard with 'the kingdom of heaven is like', which tells us that he is using it to give a lesson about the nature of the kingdom in the world.

One of God's initial plans for our world was a garden, a place of beauty and delight. Around the globe we may think of an ideal garden in different ways. If the garden has trees, they aren't grown for their timber. If there is fruit or flowers, it's not for commercial purposes. In some cases plantings are minimal, just moss or a bit of greenery contrasting with rocks, but the defined spaces are planned and tranquil.

The Persian word translated as paradise means an enclosed garden. The word is used in the Old Testament for a royal forest or an orchard. In the New Testament it refers to heaven. Jesus told the thief on the cross that he would be with him in paradise (Luke 23:43). In that paradise, living water flows and the tree of life grows with fruit in all seasons and healing leaves (Revelation 22:2).

In today's passage from Song of Songs the king compares his loved one to a set-apart garden with flowing water. He lists the exotic and valued plants to which he compares her. In *Mountains of Spices*[8], Hannah Hurnard lets the plants in verses 13 and 14 exemplify the fruit of the Spirit in our key verse. Through allegory she explains that the Holy Spirit can transform our weaknesses of temperament into their opposites and produce godly qualities. Amen!

Sorry, I am Not Available to Take Your Call

'Jesus said to Simon Peter, "Simon son of John, do you truly love me more than these?"' (John 21:15).

One night when the king stands outside his loved one's house he reveals something about himself. His head is drenched or bejewelled with dew. Some commentators aver that this points forward to Christ's agony in the Garden of Gethsemane when he grappled with the cross in lonely night-time prayer (Luke 22:44). Although Christ does not call his followers to participate in his divine act of redemption, he does ask us to identify with his suffering. His closest disciples missed their opportunity that night (Matthew 26) in the garden.

In Song of Songs, when the king calls, the woman explains, perhaps sleepily, why it's inconvenient to answer the door, hesitates and misses a singular opportunity. She is not unwilling, but slow. What the Lord asks of us may impose on our comfort zones. It is the price of our spiritual progress. Am I willing to accept what the Lord asks me to do or endure? Do I believe God will take care of the outcome for his glory?

The king even tries to assist her response, but when she awakes to the opportunity she has missed it. He has withdrawn. For the established believer, sometimes it is after we reluctantly obey that we realise what we missed by delay. It is its own rebuke. The woman says as much: 'But when I opened the door he was gone. And I died inside' (v. 6, *MSG*).

Now she calls for him, goes out to look for him. The watchmen find her. Although they hadn't rebuffed her before (3:3), now they act like Job's comforters who add injury to insult. She turns from the insensitive watchmen to the unassuming and probably less spiritually aware women, the daughters of Jerusalem. In effect she admits her failure and asks them to pray for her.

I'm grateful that at times God helps and blesses us in unexpected ways and through unexpected people. Once when I was typing at home our five-year-old son asked, 'Did you make any mistakes? I want your mistakes.' He meant the discarded carbon and tissue paper sets I used for office correspondence. Through a child the Lord said to me, 'I want your mistakes so you can start anew.'

31

Without Equal

'Yes, he is altogether lovely. This is my beloved, and this is my friend' (v.16, NKJV).

The chorus questions the woman as to how her beloved differs from others. She gives a full reply. He is radiant, the picture of health. He is outstanding, head and shoulders above others. Her testimony about him is an enthusiastic, fulsome description.

Commentators point out possible meanings of the details typifying Christ. For example, they say that 'his appearance is like Lebanon, choice as its cedars' (v. 15), meaning that even beyond his separate aspects, the effect of the Lord's total mien and stature is excellent, majestic and eternal, as symbolised by the cedars of Lebanon.

It's a song of praise. She speaks to others about him freely, frankly and with depth of feeling, assured of his approval. Her witness draws others to want to know him too. She'd hoped they would help her find him but, after praising him, when they ask her how they could find him, she knows where he is.

He's in his garden, figuratively connoting the Lord's indwelling presence in the believer. She doesn't need to go on pilgrimage or be anxious about losing a constant consciousness of his nearness. She needs quietly and confidently to wrap herself around his promise never to leave her and know he will spontaneously reveal himself to her again. He is more faithful than we are.

Through her testimony she regains her assurance. When we praise the Lord and speak about him to each other, he is near (Matthew 18:20). She has a new-found conviction. The order of her earlier declaration when she possessively said, 'He is mine and I am his' (2:16) changes to 'I am his and he is mine' (6:3).

> Loved with everlasting love,
> Led by grace that love to know;
> Spirit, breathing from above,
> Thou hast taught me this is so.
> O this full and perfect peace!
> O this transport all divine!
> In a love which cannot cease
> I am his and he is mine.
>
> *George Wade Robinson* (*SASB* 545)

Love in Action

'The LORD reigns for ever, your God, O Zion, for all generations.
Praise the LORD' (v. 10).

This is the first of the 'hallelujah psalms' (146–150), so-called because each begins and ends with the Hebrew *halelu-jah*, praise the Lord. They seem to have been written to be sung with accompaniment in the temple. All five hymns of praise have been used in daily morning synagogue services.

Someone has suggested that the five may loosely resemble the first five books of the Bible. If so, this one would correlate with Genesis.

The writer begins with a pledge to praise God for the rest of his life.

Then, perhaps realising the brevity of that life, he warns of the folly of looking to humans for help, and counsels looking to God.

The Septuagint attributes Psalm 146 to Haggai and Zechariah, which might account for the counsel in verse 3. Those prophets could have warned against trusting in rulers when they recalled that the Persian king was influenced by the enemies of the Jews and revoked his edict of support for rebuilding the walls of Jerusalem.

The God of creation is trustworthy and faithful. It is as if the psalmist gives us an outline of God's grace and righteousness: God champions the cause of the oppressed, feeds the hungry, frees the prisoner, gives sight to the blind, lifts up the bowed down, loves the righteous, preserves the alien, sustains the fatherless and the widow and turns the wicked on their heads.

Jewish hearers could illustrate how God had repeatedly done each of these throughout their history. When Jesus came, he demonstrated the same loving kindness through what some considered countercultural conduct. He asks us to follow him and encourages our creative responses.

Today may be a good time to think about how we can partner with God to show concrete care for people in need. If we ask him, God will show us practical ways of being his instruments of love, starting where we are.

———————

To ponder:

> In word and in deed
> Burning love is my need;
> I know I can find this in thee.
> *Albert Orsborn* (*SASB* 527)

The Shulammite

'. . . *dance her victory dances of love and peace*' (6:13, MSG).

Whereas the woman articulates her impressions of her loved one to others but seldom directly to him, when he speaks about her it is to her and with ease. He delights in her and says so. First he says she's as beautiful as Tirzah and as lovely as Jerusalem. Jerusalem was a place where God revealed his glory.

Tirzah was one of the cities of Canaan which Joshua conquered when the Israelites entered the Promised Land. Its name meant 'pleasant'. It must have been a choice site. After Solomon's death when the kingdom split, Tirzah became the seat of kings of the northern kingdom of Israel, as Jerusalem was of the southern kingdom of Judah.

The king iterates some of his praise of her. It helps to restore the woman's confidence and reminds us that the Lord's love never changes. The Lord restores and speaks reassurance. The other possible lesson is that what we learn at one stage of our Christian development may need to be repeated or may have richer meaning further on as our capacity to understand and incorporate revealed truth increases. In a writer's terms, one draft of a manuscript rarely suffices.

Verses 8 and 9 refer to the many and the choice one. We can understand King Solomon's frame of reference regarding women, but how does this apply to the believer? Collectively the Bride of Christ, the Church, is one body. Yet although all his followers know his love, our relationship with him differs as we each respond to his work in our individual lives. We need to appropriate willingly his grace and mercy if we want our capacity to know more of him to increase.

At the end of this chapter the woman is called Shulammite for the first time. It is the feminine form of Solomon, meaning a person of peace. Then there is a curious reference to Mahanaim, which was what Jacob named the place where he saw two angels shortly before he prepared to meet his estranged brother. Near Mahanaim he wrestled in prayer, was victorious and received his new name from the Lord, Israel. Peace and spiritual warfare are not mutually exclusive. The strength of the woman of peace is in the Lord. That's enough to make her leap for joy.

Loves Me, Loves Me, Loves Me

'How beautiful on the mountains are the feet of those who bring good news, who proclaim peace' (Isaiah 52:7).

Earlier the king praised his loved one from head to toe. Now he starts from her feet up to declare effectively his love. He sings of her graceful walk in sandalled feet (v. 1). Paul's challenge to be prepared for mission 'with your feet fitted with the readiness that comes from the gospel of peace' (Ephesians 6:15) comes to mind.

The king's descriptions of the woman also connote spiritual qualities. Her breasts may signify a mature woman capable of nourishing others. He also says that her breath exudes the scent of sweet fruit – the particular fragrance she had noted in him earlier when she delighted to sit in his shadow and eat his fruit (2:3). Verse 8 implies that she has continued to spend time with him and has become totally identified with her beloved.

In a new variation of her refrain, the woman goes further than when she initially said that he is mine and I am his (2:16), or even when she reversed the order (6:3). Now secure in his love she doesn't even mention her possession of him but emphatically asserts: I am his. I'm all the world to him (7:10). For the believer, more than what we may gain personally, living to be pleasing to the Lord is perfect preparation to be his co-worker.

They would go to the field not for her interests but his. They'd lodge in the villages as pilgrims (v. 11). They'd tend the vineyards at his pace and seek signs of fruit. In such a broadening scope of ministry to others, she could spend her life and love with and for him.

———

To ponder:

> Just where he needs me, my Lord has placed me,
> Just where he needs me, there would I be!
> And since he found me, by love he's bound me
> To serve him joyfully.
>
> *Miriam M. Richards (SASB 706)*

God's Priceless Gift

'Place me like a seal over your heart, like a seal on your arm' (v. 6).

While she waits for their wedding, the maiden wishes the king were her brother so she could show him affection. In Israel men and women did not kiss each other in public unless they were blood relatives. She wanted her inward and outward communion to fit together.

Paul expressed the Christian's dichotomy of living on this side of heaven or of Christ's return:

> We ourselves, who have the firstfruits of the Spirit, groan inwardly as we wait eagerly for our adoption as sons, the redemption of our bodies. (Romans 8:23)

But in the meantime, and it may turn out to be a considerable time, her preparation continues. 'Spiritual fitness makes us ready for his return, and this demands a close walk with the Lord.'[9]

The chorus raise the same question they asked in chapter 3 about who is coming out of the wilderness. In 8:5 they raise it specifically of the woman who appears to be leaning heavily on the king. Sometimes it takes a wilderness to remind us of how much we need the Lord.

We wonder what the woman means when she asks to be set like a seal over the king's heart and on his arm (v. 6). Is she asking him to permanently mark her image on his skin as a tattoo? Perhaps she thinks of the engraved gems on the breastpiece worn by the high priest (Exodus 28:15–21) or of signet rings pressed into wax to form official seals.

In Japan, Korea and China the hanko seal is a valuable ink stamp. The block contains characters of a person's name in a unique arrangement. The imprint proves identity, authorship or verification on documents or art. Does the woman ask the king figuratively to place the mark of her identity on his heart and arm to show he values her in his thoughts and actions?

She accounts for her request in verses 6 and 7 when she describes what she's come to understand as the nature and power of love. It is as sure and strong as death, as possessive as the grave, as passionate and blazing as intense fire (the fire flame of God), as invincible as rushing waters and absolutely priceless.

Radical Loving

'If I give all I possess to the poor and surrender my body to the flames, but have not love, I gain nothing' (1 Corinthians 13:3).

The second half of chapter 8 could be the epilogue to Song of Songs. For some commentators the book ends with verse 7 and the final verses are treated as an appendix. It starts with a flashback to the bride's younger days, then to her meeting the king.

From verse 11 onward, we return to references to a vineyard. The vineyard is let out to keepers for a thousand pieces of silver. The fruit is for the keepers' use and profit. It is up to them to tend the vineyard faithfully for their own needs and to pay the owner what is his due.

The maiden has a vineyard. Not under contract, but for the delight of service and out of love she freely gives the king what would normally be his assessment. Furthermore, she generously sees that any who help with the work are rewarded.

Her actions remind us of Zacchaeus, who proved his depth of conversion both by what he gave and how he gave it. The tax collector told the Lord that he'd give away half of his belongings to the poor. Then anything he'd gained by cheating, he would restore four times over (Luke 19:8). If we take the time to do the maths we see that by giving half away first, he ended up with less for himself in the end. Jesus knows our hearts, our motives, the depth of our love.

In songwriter Arch R. Wiggins's paraphrase of 1 Corinthians 13, he includes the line: 'My sacrifices profit me nothing unless love doth sanctify', then prays: 'Lord, in me thy love enthrone!' (*SASB* 530).

> Let me love thee, I am gladdest
> When I'm loving thee the best;
> For in sunshine or in sadness
> I can find in thee my rest.
> Love will soften every sorrow,
> Love will lighten every care,
> Love unquestioning will follow,
> Love will triumph, love will dare.
> *Herbert H. Booth* (*SASB* 503)

Chemistry and Commitment

*'After all, no-one ever hated his own body, but he feeds and cares for it,
just as Christ does the church' (v. 29).*

For generations people around the world have written love poems. They were plentiful in the Middle Eastern cultures of Bible times. Stylistically, Song of Songs is similar to others of its period. It sets the poem in the specific location of the writer. Song of Songs refers to Lebanon, Jerusalem, the Plain of Sharon, Mount Carmel and Mount Hermon as naturally as an Egyptian poem would mention the Nile.

Song of Songs also differs from poetry of its day. It assumes the theology of the Old Testament. Jews traditionally read the book on the Sabbath during Passover (this year 3 April) and hold it in high esteem – possibly to underscore God as Israel's divine husband. Some sects of Judaism read it weekly. This may correlate with Jewish teaching, which considers the Sabbath a day to enjoy physical love in marriage.

Human love is universal though expressed variously according to culture. In a way, Song of Songs is a continuation of the creation story. It shows God's endorsement of the dignity of human life and love. In a day of relative morality and casual relationships, it reminds us of the beauty of marriage. It extols the total person, spirit, mind and body, and honours winsome personalities.

From Genesis to Revelation, human sexuality is shown as a powerful gift from God. Marriage is frequently used as a metaphor to illustrate the relationship of God and his people. The book of Hosea is an example. Beneath the celebration of human love's intimacy and constancy is a spiritual meaning. The beauty of human love reflects God's love and honours him when spouses are committed to each other and to him.

We are wise to remember that our spouse cannot be God for us. On the other hand, God can be seen as the divine spouse. The Old Testament frequently mentions Israel as the wife of the Lord. The New Testament refers to the Church as the Bride of Christ and portrays the marriage supper of the Lamb as one of the ultimate events of history. Song of Songs, at the heart of the Bible, assumes a theology of God's love for his people.

More than Equal

*'There is neither Jew nor Greek, slave nor free, male nor female,
for you are all one in Christ Jesus' (Galatians 3:28).*

In 1007 a Japanese noblewoman wrote the world's first full novel, *The Tale of Genji*. The book about a prince in pursuit of love and wisdom is notable for its length and its female author. Sections of the Song of Songs may have been written or edited by a woman, or at least by someone acquainted with a woman's way of thinking.

Solomon refers to women in all three of his books. In Proverbs, a book in which Wisdom is personified, he warns of sexual entanglements and comments on marriage, then devotes the final twenty-one verses of the book in praise of a woman, a wife of noble character. In Ecclesiastes, a book in which he vacillates between faith and pessimism, Solomon presents a glum view of all of humanity, including woman.

Yet Solomon highly esteems woman in Song of Songs. The book allows for strong male and female characters, voices and points of view. He uses a women's chorus. Song of Songs does not present an aggressive male or a victimised female, but celebrates humanity, male and female, created in the image of God for mutual support.

The woman's voice is the first and last in the book and her song prevails in the drama. As the narrator, at times she reports what the man said to her. She describes the object of her love and her life's ambition to share his love, often in soliloquy.

The many references to flowers, trees and spices often connote virtues and send subtle meanings. People of the day lived more in tune with the rhythm of nature. If not just from a woman's view, such references still suggest feminine influence through the selection of illustrations. This was long before Shakespeare used flowers as symbols or *The Language of Flowers* became a standard source for Victorian flower meanings.

Song of Songs hints at the value of woman. Someone has said the emancipation of women began when Christ ushered woman into a new place in human relations by according her a dignity she'd never known before. We think of women he healed or helped, who supported his ministry, who were the first to see him after his resurrection. Men and women are viewed as one in Christ.

Love in Action

*'The LORD upholds all those who fall and lifts up all
who are bowed down' (v. 14).*

Have you ever been part of a feeding ministry? In January 1937 during
the worst flood in Ohio's history, my father's mother first became
involved with The Salvation Army when she volunteered to supervise its
food services for flood victims who were temporarily housed in a school.

In addition to times of natural disasters, feeding ministries have
provided essential sustenance for people in times of war, economic
distress, unemployment and homelessness. The Church has a long history
of helping the needy.

All four Gospels relate Jesus' use of minimal resources to feed crowds of
thousands. No doubt we think about those instances when we help
distribute countless tins of food and loaves of bread. In some cities, rest-
aurants partner with concerned citizens to move leftover food to feeding
programmes – many of which are run from kitchens of faith-based
agencies.

Some congregations have provided meals for decades. Workers in
Salvation Army street feeding ministries – from Tokyo, Japan, to Santiago,
Chile – take hot food to locations where people in need congregate on cold
nights. Often such schemes lead to identifying other basic human needs or
advocating for change.

Jesus launched his ministry in a synagogue in Nazareth when he stood
and read prophetic portions from Isaiah which pertained to him. Besides
being anointed to preach the gospel to the poor, he said he was sent to
announce release, recovery and deliverance to 'those who are oppressed
[who are downtrodden, bruised, crushed, and broken down by calamity]'
(Luke 4:18, *AB*).

Whether we scoop soup from five-gallon buckets into individual portion
containers, wash and cut vegetables for a hearty stew, boil pounds of rice
or pasta, prepare sandwiches or lend practical support in other ways, there
is something for willing hands to do to help. Prayer for the helpers and the
helped is also vital.

Whether it's Poverty and Homeless Action Week where we live or not,
we can ask God to show us what action we can take to be partners in
upholding those who are downtrodden.

Feet Speak

God moves in a mysterious way
His wonders to perform;
He plants his footsteps in the sea
And rides upon the storm.
William Cowper (*SASB* 29)

Introduction

Moved by muscles and tendons, held together by ligaments, the foot's twenty-six bones are covered by a glove of skin. If chopsticks are said to be graceful extensions of the hand, are shoes containers for the humble foot?

Shop window displays of women's shoes usually feature small sizes. This isn't new. Heels came into vogue in the 1500s because they were thought to make feet look smaller, and small feet have generally been thought more attractive. However, smaller feet have some disadvantages. Think physics. A smaller base gives less structural support. The phrase 'sensible shoes' says it all.

Shoes feature in a number of cultural sayings. For example, there's the Native American adage, 'Never judge a man until you walk a mile in his moccasins.' In *To Kill a Mockingbird*, the main character says, 'Atticus was right. One time he said you never really know a man until you stand in his shoes and walk around in them.'

Feet, footwear, footsteps and walking are frequently used in Scripture, from Genesis to Revelation, both literally and metaphorically. For example: 'Whether you turn to the right or to the left, your ears will hear a voice behind you, saying, "This is the way; walk in it"' (Isaiah 30:21); 'I want you to get out there and walk – better yet, run! – on the road God called you to travel. I don't want anyone strolling off, down some path that goes nowhere' (Ephesians 4:1, *MSG*).

We'll consider a few ways that the lowly foot teaches lofty lessons.

Designed for Heights

'The Sovereign LORD is my strength; he makes my feet like the feet of a deer, he enables me to go on the heights' (v. 19).

Televised dance competitions capture attention. The eye-catching costumes may add pizzazz, but are minor elements compared with the timing and limber moves that win judges' approval. The dancers' agility depends on their trained feet. Leonardo da Vinci called the foot 'a masterpiece of engineering and a work of art'.

Last week we mentioned the Shulammite's victory dance (Song of Songs 6:13), implying the skilful use of her feet, and in the next chapter the king's praise of her graceful walk. Even the king in Song of Songs was described as leaping over hills and mountains like the deer, implying confidence and nimbleness. Split-toed animals can be extremely sure-footed.

What we stand on matters too. The soles of our feet are designed with nerves that communicate data to other parts of our bodies. They register what we're walking on, whether plush grass, hot sand, firm pavement or wet stones, and they help keep us stable.

In his brief book, the prophet Habakkuk cries out to the Lord about perceived injustice. God gives him a revelation of his plan to deal with that injustice and instructs Habakkuk to write the revelation down so legibly and plainly that anyone who reads it can understand it and share the good news of coming deliverance.

In the final chapter the prophet confidently announces that even though he does not yet see evidence of blessing replacing blight, he will rejoice in God with the certainty that the Lord who is his strength and 'has made my feet like hinds' feet, makes me walk on my high places' (v. 19, *NASB*). That version points toward a customised, personal journey – preparing my feet for my walk on my high places.

The Holy Spirit is willing as we ask him. We pray:

> Lord, lift me up and let me stand
> By faith on Heaven's tableland:
> A higher plane than I have found;
> Lord, plant my feet on higher ground.
> *Johnson Oatman, Jr (SASB chorus 80)*

By Foot

'Their feet touched the water's edge, the water from upstream stopped flowing' (vv. 15, 16).

That feet play an important role in Scripture is little wonder since the average person's main means of travel in Bible times was by foot. When the Hebrews left Egypt, 'There were about six hundred thousand men on foot, besides women and children' (Exodus 12:37). We all depend on our feet to some extent, but even in our day millions still rely exclusively on foot travel.

God told Abraham, Moses and Joshua what the scope of the Israelites' Promised Land would be. He delineated the boundaries to the new leader, Joshua: 'I will give you every place where you set your foot, as I promised Moses' (Joshua 1:3).

When Joshua prepared the people to cross the Jordan River, he told them that the sign that God was with them and would drive out their enemies ahead of them would be that when the feet of the priests who carried the ark of the Lord touched the river, the water from upstream would stop flowing. This must have seemed impossible with the Jordan at flood stage.

Yet it happened and the people all hurried across the dry river bed. Each one passed the priests who stood on dry ground in the middle of the river holding the ark. The drama wasn't over. God instructed that twelve stones from the place where the priests stood be retrieved for a memorial to God's provision.

Only after that did God at last command the priests to come out of the river. 'No sooner had they set their feet on the dry ground than the waters of the Jordan returned to their place and ran in flood as before' (Joshua 4:18).

We can imagine that everyone who strode across the Jordan had a story to tell future generations, but none more than the priests whose obedience and faith in action found their feet to be God's instruments that day.

Our feet may never be tested the way the priests' were, but is there some way our feet can demonstrate our obedience and faith too? Has the Lord asked us to visit someone, to stand in some form of public witness, to return an overpayment, or in some other way to use our feet as his followers? He will use us if we're willing.

Divinely Durable

'Observe the commands of the LORD your God, walking in his ways and revering him' (v. 6).

In certain countries, people traditionally remove their shoes at home. It may be for cleanliness, convenience or comfort. It may not have been customary for the Israelites to wear shoes at home in Egypt. But they ate their last evening meal with their shoes on.

Moses conveyed the Lord's instructions: 'This is how you are to eat it: with your cloak tucked into your belt, your sandals on your feet and your staff in your hand. Eat it in haste; it is the LORD's Passover' (Exodus 12:11). We know now that they were about to embark on an unusual and lengthy journey. Their feet would need protection.

Forty years and many miles later Moses reminds the new generation of God's instructions and the way the Lord led their parents on the night they fled from Egypt and continued to lead his people up to their current location just east of the Jordan River. They were poised to enter the Promised Land.

He recalls that by God's miraculous provision they were fed throughout their journey through inhospitable wilderness. We remember the daily manna. But something else Moses points out is just as wonderful: 'During the forty years that I led you through the desert, your clothes did not wear out, nor did the sandals on your feet' (Deuteronomy 29:5). In another place he says that their feet didn't even swell. Had they realised God's provision?

God takes care of the details. Sometimes we can see it in retrospect, but often we aren't aware of all he does for us as we follow him. We pause to think about how God has answered prayer, but what about the ways he's provided for us beyond our asking?

When I ask a particular friend how he is, he often replies: 'I'm better than I deserve to be.' Considering God's care for us can be humbling. We don't deserve his love, grace, mercy or any other of his generous gifts. When contemplating God's pinnacle of love, the sacrifice of Christ on the cross, hymnwriter Isaac Watts wrote:

> Love so amazing, so divine,
> Demands my soul, my life, my all.
> (*SASB* 136)

Foot Care

'If you have realised these things, you will find your happiness in doing them' (v. 17, JBP).

In the Middle East, open sandals and travel by foot made washing one's feet or having them washed welcome refreshment. It was part of usual hospitality to provide water for the purpose. Abraham offered water so the strangers who visited him could wash (Genesis 18). Joseph had water offered to his estranged brothers for the same purpose (Genesis 43). Per God's instruction to Moses, the basin placed in the tabernacle courtyard was a place for Moses and the priests to wash their hands and feet whenever they entered to serve God or approach the altar.

When Simon criticised the woman who washed Jesus' feet with her tears, Jesus not only forgave her sins but also reproved his host for not providing water for his feet (Luke 7). Yet rather than washing their own feet or having a servant assist, at the Last Supper Jesus chose to wash his disciples' feet as an expression of love and humility. Some churches conduct a foot-washing service on Maundy Thursday. They commemorate Jesus' action and his charge to wash each other's feet.

Some still find the literal observance of his charge important. Some denominations observe it regularly as an act of humility, commitment and egalitarianism. The act is rooted in love. A friend told me that she knew what love was when she saw her brother massaging his wife's deformed, aching feet. In a related vein, there is a club which meets to share a meal and then shine each other's shoes, serving each other in bare feet.

A famed Italian shoe designer who finds feet very telling was asked how she became interested in making men's shoes. She replied that around the time of the Second World War, when she was cared for at a convent, one day she stood in front of a picture of the crucifixion. Since she was small, her eyes were close to the bottom of the picture, at the level of Christ's pierced feet. She decided she would learn how to take the nails out, the pain out of men's feet, and devote her life to it.

———————

To ponder:

How can I humbly serve another Christian this week?

Walking Aids

*'For you have delivered me from death and my feet from stumbling,
that I may walk before God in the light of life' (v. 13).*

Modern versions of mukluks will be popular souvenir footwear from the 2010 Winter Olympics in British Columbia, Canada. The soft-soled calf-high boots follow Arctic aboriginal design. Traditionally they were made of reindeer or seal skin lined with fur. They weigh little and allow hunters to pursue prey quietly. They are ideal for crossing snow, but are not really suitable for hard pavements.

Isabel Crawford, a missionary to Native North Americans, paraphrased Psalm 23:4:

> Sometime, it may be very soon, it may be a long, long time, He will draw me into a valley. It is dark there, but I'll be afraid not, for it is in between those mountains that the Shepherd Christ will meet me and the hunger that I have in my heart all through this life will be satisfied. He gives me a staff to lean upon.

Psalm 23 focuses on the presence of the shepherd, but includes what he provides – among other things a staff. Stability when walking is important and those who lack it require various aids. Even with a walking stick, it was difficult for me to manage trails on rocky hills until I bought wide-based, well-built walking shoes for balance. Careful choice of shoes – or in the case of the Winter Olympic competitions, skates and ski boots – can also be important for support.

God offers us spiritual trainers that help us keep our balance in our Christian walk. Keeping conscious of his word is vital. 'The law of his God is in his heart; his feet do not slip' (Psalm 37:31). We read Scripture and sometimes memorise special verses or listen to Scripture-based music.

Prayer and praise are another form of spiritual footgear and they're always within reach. When we remember that God rescued us from sin and gave us solid footing, we rejoice. When we think we're nearly losing our footing and pray to be restored to firm faith, God answers. When we walk in his way and count on his promise: 'He will guard the feet of his saints' (1 Samuel 2:9), we know the assurance of God's blessing and peace.

Removing Shoes

' "*We are witnesses. May the LORD make the woman who is coming into your home like Rachel and Leah, who together built up the house of Israel. May you have standing in Ephrathah and be famous in Bethlehem*" ' (v. 11).

In certain Salvation Army corps (churches) in Japan the entryway walls are lined with shoebox-size compartments full of matching leatherette slippers stamped with the corps' name. We removed our shoes and replaced them with a pair of the communal slippers as we entered, and reversed the process when we left.

We thought about shepherd Moses seeing a burning bush and hearing God's voice. He received divine instruction to remove his sandals because he was standing on holy ground (Exodus 3). Moses' successor, Joshua, had a similar encounter and instruction before the battle of Jericho (Joshua 5).

In some Middle Eastern countries, entering a place of worship with shoes on is an insult. There, removing shoes signals reverence, hospitality, humility, mourning or endorsement of a contract.

The story of the young widow from Moab whose faithfulness to her mother-in-law gave rise to her new faith and life in her adopted land of Israel is legendary. When bachelor Boaz realised that he could purchase Naomi's property and marry Ruth if their nearer eligible relative declined, he went to the town gate where public business was transacted.

The closer relative wanted the property, but not the woman. '(Now in earlier times in Israel, for the redemption and transfer of property to become final, one party took off his sandal and gave it to the other. This was the method of legalising transactions in Israel.) So the kinsman-redeemer said to Boaz, "Buy it yourself." And he removed his sandal' (Ruth 4:7, 8).

So their engagement was sealed with a shoe. No doubt the memory of that shoe held as much significance for Ruth as a ring or other gift in pledge of marriage holds for women today. On top of the blessing of marriage, Ruth and Boaz's great-grandson would be David, king of Israel and an ancestor of Jesus Christ.

———————

To ponder:

What everyday action can remind me of whose I am?

God Comes in Majesty

'The Almighty is beyond our reach and exalted in power' (Job 37:23).

The first eleven verses of Psalm 147 are attributed to Haggai and Zechariah – prophets during the time of the Israelites' return from exile and period of rebuilding. The psalm calls the returnees and us to sing praise and thanksgiving to God for his providence, his provision, his peace and his power.

At certain times, such as the run-up to Christmas or Valentine's Day, radio advertisements urge listeners to name stars after people. For a fee, an international registry or an online site records the named star. The name is not recognised by astronomers or others in the scientific community, but the giver and recipient are satisfied that in the vastness of space with its innumerable stars they have personalised and taken vicarious possession of a heavenly body.

Verse 4 of today's psalm reminds us that the Lord, Creator of the universe, has first call on the number and names of the stars. God can count the stars even if the smartest person or most complex computer can't manage it.

What is truly immeasurable is his understanding (v. 5). The psalmists illustrate that point by noting an unexpected display of grace – God's support of those who are meek, humble or afflicted (v. 6). Furthermore, they say that all living creatures, especially the young and helpless, depend on God for sustenance. In fact, rather than the kinds of things which please humankind, God simply delights in all who trust him and hope in his love.

In verses 8, 9 and 14 to 18 we notice the many references to God's care in nature – from elements of the water cycle to the winter snow, frost, hail and wind. It's interesting that the writers connect some of these with God broadcasting his word.

A similar passage in Job says: 'God's voice thunders in marvellous ways; he does great things beyond our understanding. He says to the snow, "Fall on the earth" . . . The breath of God produces ice, and the broad waters become frozen' (Job 37:5, 6, 10).

If while watching the Olympic events in their snowy panorama surrounding Vancouver, Canada, we pause to praise the Creator for both his works and his Word, we'll know a richer meaning to the motto of the twenty-first Winter Olympics, 'With glowing hearts'.

Where Do We Stand?

'Let us go to his dwelling-place; let us worship at his footstool' (Psalm 132:7).

Travellers consider it an inconvenience or an indignity to remove shoes in public, but today airport security demands it. In some places it is considered rude to show the soles of one's feet to others, even accidentally. An uncovered foot can be offensive. Might Paul have had the foot in mind when he wrote about treating some parts of the body with modesty (v. 23)?

In Thailand it is an extreme insult for the foot, socks or shoes to touch or be placed over someone's head. The journalist who hurled his shoes at President Bush at a Baghdad press conference meant to insult him.

We often speak of something underfoot negatively, as an impediment to progress. In Scripture when we read about things that are underfoot, usually it is in the sense of under authority. Psalm 8:6 says that God made human beings the rulers over his creation and put everything on earth under our feet.

God describes heaven as his throne and the earth as his footstool (Isaiah 66:1). When Jesus quotes what David writes of God making his anointed one's enemies his footstool (Psalm 110) we understand that he means the Messiah's ultimate triumph.

Zechariah speaks of the day of the Lord with the specific detail that his feet will again stand on the Mount of Olives – the place where Christ stood with his disciples when he ascended.

In Ezekiel when the glory of the Lord filled the temple, the prophet heard the divine message: 'Son of man, this is the place of my throne and the place for the soles of my feet. This is where I will live among the Israelites for ever' (Ezekiel 43:7).

Psalm 132 remembers King David's zeal and initial effort to restore the ark of the covenant to a permanent place of honour and worship, all of which revived the people's determination to worship God 'at his footstool'.

How do we join such worship? We come closer to his footstool by exalting the Lord in our corporate and private worship, in our hearts and through holy living. If we ask him, he will show us how.

To Have and to Hold

'He threw himself at Jesus' feet and thanked him – and he was a Samaritan'
(Luke 17:16).

When a car is parked illegally, local authorities sometimes immobilise it with a locking wheel clamp so it stays in place until a fine is paid. In certain contact sports, players try to prevent opponents from moving the ball forward by grabbing and holding the player's legs. But it's not an appropriate method for gaining or keeping someone's attention in normal daily life.

On the first Easter, the women who meet Jesus as they leave the empty tomb clasp his feet and worship him. They thought they had lost him, but now that he is with them again they don't want to let him go.

When a woman's only child dies, desperate for help she travels quickly to Mount Carmel to the prophet she knows serves God. Nothing can keep her from imploring Elisha for help in person. When she reaches him at the mountain she seizes his feet, frantically questioning her loss. She will return home only if he goes with her, which he does. Her son's restoration from death tops all previous divine blessings. When she sees her boy alive again, out of overwhelming gratitude her first impulse is to bow to the ground at the prophet's feet. Only then does she take her child back.

Holding another's feet suggests desperation. Bowing at someone's feet displays complete subservience and deep respect. Western culture has its formal bows from head, waist or knee, but Eastern culture has perfected the full-body bow, the lower the more respectful. To execute it gracefully takes practice.

It might not be polished, but the type of bow the one grateful leper displays when he realises he's been healed and returns to thank Jesus (Luke 17:15–16) involves his whole body and soul.

———

To pray:

> At thy feet I bow adoring,
> Bending lower, lower still;
> Giving up my all to follow,
> Just to do my Master's will.
>
> *Susie Barker* (*SASB* chorus 35)

If Shoes Could Talk

'But the father said to his servants, "Quick! Bring the best robe and put it on him. Put a ring on his finger and sandals on his feet" ' (v. 22).

A master cobbler can read much from the wear and tear of shoes brought in for repair. Shoes can tell stories. The film, *Tree of Wooden Clogs*, describes peasant life in an Italian village in the 1800s. It focuses on the poor and their shoes. In Holocaust museums, the piles of shoes are some of the most powerful images – tangible evidence of nameless victims who walk history's silent halls.

At some point in the American Civil War, store owners were in a quandary when their shops were suddenly overrun by armed men who helped themselves to boots and shoes before inspecting other goods. Footgear was prized even above such essentials as food.

During a period of prayer I was surprised to hear a young adult thanking God that she had shoes on her feet. Although she was born in the USA, her family had escaped Khmer Rouge persecution in Cambodia. She would be able to appreciate the plight of children in New England mill towns of the early 1900s who took turns wearing shared shoes, and often saved them for Sundays.

The prophet Amos records God's displeasure with Israel's neighbours and with Israel for breaking covenant with him. Social injustice is at such a low point that the poor are abused, their essential garments which are taken in collateral are flagrantly used to carpet places of idol worship and the needy are sold into slavery for debts as minor as the price of a pair of sandals (Amos 2:6–8).

We see a powerful contrast to this behaviour in the finale of Jesus' story of the prodigal son. The magnanimous father greets his repentant son with warmth and forgiveness. He offers restoration at every level (Luke 15:20ff.). The barefoot vagabond undeservedly receives what he lost through his wrong choices – family, clothes and shoes, dignity, respect and food. Every step he takes in his new shoes reminds him of what he's gained, but even more of the love of his father who made it possible.

Can something as simple remind me of God's provision? As we begin Lent, what daily blessing tells me of my Father's great love?

In Jesus' Steps

'Then the angel said to him, "Put on your clothes and sandals."
And Peter did so' (v. 8).

When we think of shoes we think also of socks. Historically, they came along much later and probably started as boot linings made of natural materials such as cloth, animal skin or matted hair. Fragments of knitted socks from the second century have been found in Syria.

An unusual sock art rug designed and woven by Elizabeth Cousins, *Old Sock, Odd Sock, Big Weave*, is displayed in St Mary's Church, Hadlow, Kent, England. The image portrays the globe and is made from socks donated by local residents, friends, relatives and visitors. The socks represent everyday things we use with little thought. Each contribution makes a difference to the final work and points to our interdependence.

Made of natural and manufactured fibres, the socks provoke questions about how and where they were produced and at what cost to those involved or to the environment. Since socks imply feet, they can symbolise our footsteps, the choices we make, the paths we take through life.

Herod arrested, persecuted and killed some of the leaders of the early Church. He had Peter put in prison, intending to put him on trial immediately after Passover. The night before the trial, as Peter slept in chains without shoes or coat, the cell suddenly lit up. An angel told Peter to put on his shoes, wrap his cloak around him and follow him out.

Peter could hardly believe his deliverance until in the middle of the night he'd walked the length of one street, perhaps hearing only his own footsteps. When the angel left, Peter hurried to a place where he knew believers gathered so he could give them evidence of God's answer to their prayers.

This may have been one experience which later prompted Peter to urge believers to respectfully submit to unfair suffering and demonstrate God's grace when he wrote: 'To this you were called, because Christ suffered for you, leaving you an example, that you should follow in his steps' (1 Peter 2:21).

We want our testimony to be: 'My feet have closely followed his steps; I have kept to his way without turning aside' (Job 23:11).

The Mark in a Footstep

'Since we live by the Spirit, let us keep in step with the Spirit' (v. 25).

We walk along wet sand at low tide and see the trail our footprints leave. Fresh snow shows signs of early risers – the footprints of birds and animals whose trails are otherwise invisible. Other than those cast in plaster for posterity, footprints are generally short-lived. God's are not seen at all, yet we see evidence of his presence.

The psalmist recalls God's deliverance of the Israelites from Egypt: 'Your path led through the sea, your way through the mighty waters, though your footprints were not seen' (Psalm 77:19). After the exodus, when God called Moses, Aaron, Aaron's sons and seventy elders of Israel to the mountain, being in his presence was so wonderful that they could only describe the pavement beneath God's 'feet', which was like sapphire or lapis lazuli, clear blue as the sky (Exodus 24:10).

The well-known poem, 'Footprints', details a man's dream about looking back on his life's path and seeing two sets of footprints, his and the Lord's. He is dismayed that at difficult times there is only one set of prints and questions the Lord about leaving him alone at such times. The Lord's reply is that he never left him. When there was only one set of prints it was because God was carrying him.

Job complained that God put marks on the soles of his feet to be able to track his paths (13:27). What would he think of today's surveillance techniques? Later Job sees things from a new perspective and asserts confidently: 'But he knows the way that I take; when he has tested me, I will come forth as gold' (23:10).

A three-year-old may shuffle around the house in his dad's slippers and momentarily feel 'grown-up' until he trips. An assistant may be called on to temporarily take over for an ailing superior and feel privileged or overwhelmed in turn.

Paul knew the privilege and humiliation of walking in Jesus' footsteps. He wrote to the Galatians: 'Finally, let no-one cause me trouble, for I bear on my body the marks of Jesus' (6:17). We're reminded that we follow the Christ who endured the physical suffering of the cross for us. During Lent as we retrace his footsteps to the cross we may want to consider whether those who come behind us can recognise the marks of Jesus in our footsteps.

Walking Together

*'And a highway will be there; it will be called the Way of Holiness.
The unclean will not journey on it; it will be for those
who walk in that Way' (v. 8).*

One of my friends does not take a walk unless it's a means to her destination. Others walk whenever the weather allows whether through the neighbourhood or along a favourite path. Physical disabilities could make any type of walk for pleasure a challenge.

Even worse, self-inflicted disabilities of spirit brought on by selfishness and sin make traversing inhospitable wilderness situations troublesome. Isaiah 35 says that God wants to turn our spiritual deserts into places of lush abundance. Further, he offers to restore spiritual sight, hearing and an easy gait to those who choose his way. But this isn't just so we can enjoy the restored environment and set up house there.

God wants us to live with him. How do we get to his dwelling, the Holy City, the Zion of God (v. 10)? We walk there with him, at his pace and as he directs. As long as we stay on his pedestrian highway, there will be no potholes to trip us up or beasts to overwhelm us. The only thing we can expect to overtake us is gladness and joy.

In more than half the books of the Bible, life with God is described as a walk. Both Noah and his great-grandfather Enoch were said to have walked with God. It's no surprise that God asks his people 'to fear the LORD your God, to walk in all his ways, to love him, to serve the LORD your God with all your heart and with all your soul' (Deuteronomy 10:12).

Not only should they walk with him, but God promises that if Israel will follow him and obey him, he will put his dwelling place among them and walk among them and be their God, and they his people (Leviticus 26:12). It's a mutual walk.

In his book, *Walking With God*,[10] author W. Phillip Keller says that walking together with God suggests having a friendship with God characterised by the benefits brought by harmony, sharing, learning, exercise, separation, inspiration, destination, new heights and a profound awareness of how good the good news is. Best of all, we even become more like the one with whom we walk. Amen!

A Pedestrian's Prayer

'Show me the way I should go, for to you I lift up my soul' (v. 8).

Sometimes when we're desperate, we naturally pray for release from our trouble. In Psalm 143 David prefaces his prayer for deliverance with a request for God's mercy and forgiveness. In other places he asks God to take note of his innocence, but here he acknowledges humanity's condition and his own unworthiness before the All-Holy.

He remembers what God has done for him in the past and reaches out for God as parched lands do for refreshing rains. His prayer is urgent. God is his only hope. Those who know drought stay keenly sensitive to the faintest scent, smallest cloud or slightest draught – that hint of longed-for rain. The psalmist asks that, because he trusts God, the morning will bring word of his unfailing, loving kindness.

In verses 8 to 10 the writer uses progress by foot as a metaphor for guidance, a pedestrian's prayer: 'Show me where to *walk*, for I give myself to you. I *run* to you to hide me. Teach me to do your will, for you are my God. May your gracious Spirit *lead me forward on a firm footing*' (*NLT*).

Years ago, when I was in college and seeking spiritual certainty, I read a poem titled 'Meadowland' by Daisy M. Polhamus. God used it to bring me the assurance I needed. The author described walking through a narrow ditch so deep that she could barely see the sky overhead. She'd heard that it would open into meadowland, but had walked in the ditch for so long she'd begun to wonder if it was true or if it would lead her underground.

Then the Lord whispered to her that he too had walked in a narrow and deep pathway and found it hard when he was left alone. He reminded her that he did it for her and was with her now even in this ditch. He asked her if she could trust him. The trekker replied, 'Yes, Lord, I will, Lord, forever! And you know, I think I can smell the meadowland!'

To pray:

'Teach me to do your will, for you are my God; may your good Spirit lead me on level ground' (v. 10).

Letters from a Missionary

Introduction

Before the days of email, when long-distance telephone calls were expensive, people relied more on the post for communication. Thin airmail stationery maximised the number of pages one could write. Wordy correspondents filled the onionskin pages, then turned them sideways and wrote perpendicularly across the initial paragraphs in a different colour of ink.

I often wrote via the blue aerogramme. They were first issued in the 1930s in Iraq, but popularised internationally in the 1940s. In many countries the price of the single sheet of lightweight paper included the postage. The page was folded in thirds, flaps sealed and the outside addressed, with no enclosures allowed. Although I haven't received or sent one in a long time, for about thirty years the blue air letter was the main way our family kept in touch.

Nearly two thousand years ago, the apostle Paul wrote lengthier hand-delivered letters to believers. Many letters, such as 1 Corinthians, were to people he had introduced to Christ. He wrote to encourage or correct them, to request their prayers or to thank them for their gifts.

Paul established the church in Corinth on his second missionary journey and wrote to believers there several times. The city of Corinth was known for brazen immorality. The society the Christians lived in prized the wrong things and held antithetical views to those of the gospel. Paul longed for believers to develop a mindset that would keep them from caving in to the skewed thinking that surrounded them.

Although not initially addressed to us, we find Paul's letters relevant to our day. We view them in the context of their time and purpose. As part of Scripture, God speaks truth to us through them.

To God's Boundless Community of Saints

'I include in my greeting all who call out to Jesus, wherever they live.
He's their Master as well as ours!' (v. 2, MSG).

I've written letters on aircraft and in hotel rooms, in a baseball stadium, during conferences, on a summer porch or next to a winter fire. My location quite possibly affected some of what I wrote. Other than something dire, setting doesn't appear to play much of a role in the style of letters prevalent in Paul's day. Rather, his letters to fellow believers follow a mode of writing to acquaintances common to his era. He identifies himself and greets the recipients, prays for their well-being, expresses gratitude, gives his message, and closes with personal notes and regards.

He does not set out to write doctrinal treatises but, as a pastor, deals with troublesome situations. He writes out of necessity and from wherever he may be – not from the quiet of a private study or library. In the period's customary method, he uses a secretary to write what he dictates. We can imagine him pacing as he does so.

Paul wrote several letters to the Christians in Corinth. Scholars think these probably numbered four and that they are now combined into 1 and 2 Corinthians. Paul wrote most of Corinthians from Ephesus, the only city during his missionary journeys where he stayed longer than he did at Corinth.

Paul starts his letter by briefly noting his credentials – God called him to be an apostle of Christ. He also includes a name we see only here in the letter, Sosthenes, possibly his scribe. He may have been the man mentioned in Acts 18, a ruler of the Corinthian synagogue. He was the one the Jews beat in front of the Roman court for allowing Paul to preach at their synagogue. Evidently he became a Christian.

When Paul mentions Sosthenes as a companion at the opening of the letter, he connects with the Corinthian Christians. It is also significant that in the opening three verses of the letter, Paul mentions the name Jesus Christ four times (or five if we count 'Lord'). Rather than from his own opinions or human regulations, Paul's appeal will be through the love of Christ.

Note that Paul writes to the church of God in Corinth, not to the church of Corinth. He emphasises that they, along with all Christians everywhere, are in Christ and are called to holiness.

Gifted

'Therefore you do not lack any spiritual gift as you eagerly wait for our Lord Jesus Christ to be revealed. He will keep you strong to the end, so that you will be blameless on the day of our Lord Jesus Christ' (vv. 7, 8).

Paul begins by being thankful for his readers and the promised grace Christ has given them. He congratulates them that since he first introduced them to the gospel, they'd been enriched by sound preaching and their resulting knowledge. This gains him a hearing since Paul knows they pride themselves in these. It also prepares them for what he will say later about their abuse of such valued speech and knowledge.

Paul reminds them that they have been gifted, as have we. Our chief gift through the grace and love of God is salvation through Christ. Other gifts equip us for living to glorify God.

'Spiritual gifts' that Paul focuses on later in his letter – such as preaching, healing, helping, teaching, giving, faith, prophecy, hospitality, administration, discernment, leadership and languages – fit us to serve the body of Christ.

But there are other gifts we enjoy which can be developed to serve God and humankind. We benefit from all craftsmen, artists, musicians, cooks, writers, athletes, actors, farmers, teachers, health professionals, architects and others who hold their skills in trust, develop them and employ them in God-directed ways.

Paul reminds us that Christ has furnished us with the graces and gifts we need and he will keep us strong to the end. I frequently need to be reminded of this. Because God called Christians in Corinth into fellowship with Christ, and God is faithful, Paul does not doubt the outcome if they continue to follow Christ as Lord.

In his song, 'Give me a restful mind' (*SASB* 574), songwriter Frederick George Hawkes asks God for the peace of a restful mind, the assurance of a trustful mind, the God-honouring service of an earnest mind, the endurance of a steadfast mind and the fullness of praise to the Lord that issues from a thankful mind. Such gifts can help ground our lives as Christians. Let's ask God for them.

Is Christ Divided?

'Let there be no divisions in the Church' (v. 10, NLT).

Paul leads naturally from reminding the Corinthians both of God's faithfulness in their past and his continued provision as basis of hope for their future into an appeal to them to sort out their differences in the present. He doesn't order them to fall into place, but addresses them with love and equality as siblings.

For some reason factions had developed. People lined up with their favourite leader – Apollos, Peter, Paul or Christ. Those whose jerseys said 'Follow Paul' were likely mostly Gentiles who may have turned Paul's message of freedom into licence.

Apollos was a Jew from Alexandria, a city of intellectuals. Those who wore 'Follow Apollo' jerseys may have enjoyed intellectualising their faith. And the 'Follow Peter' crowd were probably Jews who were proponents of rituals and rules, legalists. If another group claimed to be the only true followers of Christ, their exclusivity would have been self-righteousness.

Paul calls them to harmony in the name of the incomparable Christ. For the tenth time in as many verses, Paul refers to Christ. Who else could be both the centre and the source of Christian unity? Early church father Chrysostom reflected that since the apostle uses the name of Christ more often in 1 Corinthians than in any other Epistle, Paul apparently wants to draw his readers' focus to Christ alone.

Paul doesn't disparage diversity, but entreats believers to aim at unity and to make allowance for each other's differences. He asks them not only to come to agreement, but also to be mended the way a broken bone or a wound heals and binds together for the good of the body.

Paul's comments about baptism do not belittle meaningful public witnesses to inward grace. It is important to declare our faith and intention as believers. Rather, Paul is relieved that he'd baptised few of the Corinthians lest people think he'd baptised converts for a 'Follow Paul' group. He knew that his primary commission was pointing to the cross and preaching the gospel for a verdict.

To ponder:

Does my Christian identity point to Christ?

Cross Wise

'For the foolishness of God is wiser than man's wisdom, and the weakness of God is stronger than man's strength' (v. 25).

In her assignment to write a poem full of emotion, a fellow student on my poetry course bitterly denounced the statues of her childhood religious teaching. She'd been taught to trust them for help and they'd failed her. She couldn't look beyond the icons, so she scrapped her faith along with them. With similar misplaced trust in traditions and presumptions, Paul says that the Jews and the Greeks couldn't see why a Messiah, sent by God, then crucified and resurrected in fulfilment of prophecy, should be the object of religion, much less require personal repentance.

The Jews who looked for a conquering hero could not embrace a suffering servant even though the prophet Isaiah wrote of such a Messiah (Isaiah 53). They sought spectacular signs and wonders, not a King on a cross. They couldn't comprehend God's plan of salvation through Christ's death.

The Greeks who held that a God who suffered was an oxymoron denounced a suffering Saviour. They were enamoured with the concept of wisdom, admired oratory and held stimulating discussions just for mental exercise. They loved big words. They could not handle the simplicity of the Christian message. To them it lacked polish, didn't command respect and seemed foolish.

But there were Jews and Greeks who dared to believe the gospel in the earliest days of the Church, and for them Christ was the power and wisdom of God. Today there are people who have been inclined against believing the gospel of God in Christ by biases as entrenched as those of the early Jews and Greeks, but who have come to a personal knowledge of him.

Paul did not consider God or his ways foolish or weak, rather he knew that even what people deemed divine weakness was far greater than all human wisdom or strength (v. 25).

———————

To pray:

> **Lord, give us light thy truth to see,**
> **And make us wise in knowing thee.**
> *Thomas Benson Pollack (SASB 466)*

A Cross-shaped Mindset

'God has united you with Christ Jesus. For our benefit God made him to be wisdom itself. Christ made us right with God; he made us pure and holy, and he freed us from sin' (v. 30, NLT).

At one time, when 'wise' as a suffix was in style, a cartoon showed a fledgling owl, his parent and teacher in a classroom. The parent said, 'I know how he's doing sport-wise and art-wise, but how is he doing wise-wise?'

Paul states that by human standards, not many of the Corinthian believers were wise, influential or of noble birth. But God was in the habit of choosing just those things people judged to be of little value or power to display his ability, even bringing something out of nothing (vv. 27–29). Paul implies that not only did the Creator make the world from nothing, but when God brought the church in Corinth into being, it too was something out of nothing.

God often chooses to use what most consider the ordinary rather than the exceptional and surprises us by turning societal norms upside down. Paul sensed that if the Corinthians would think about the way God works, it could help to straighten out those who wanted to align with particular wise or powerful leaders. Contrary to those seeking status or party affiliation in the Church, Jesus intentionally lowered his status for our sakes.

We don't understand why, but God revealed the great plan of salvation to simple believers. In Matthew 11:25, 26 Jesus thanked God for choosing to do this: 'I praise you, Father, Lord of heaven and earth, because you have hidden these things from the wise and learned, and revealed them to little children.'

Someone has called Christ's self-giving love the cross-shaped mindset of God's holiness. Paul points out that Christ, who has become the wisdom of God for us, is our righteousness, our holiness and our redemption.

He closes with the reminder from Jeremiah 9:24: 'But those who wish to boast should boast in this alone: that they truly know me and understand that I am the Lord who demonstrates unfailing love and who brings justice and righteousness to the earth, and that I delight in these things.' May that be our honest testimony today!

Persuasion versus Demonstration

'So that your faith might not rest on men's wisdom,
but on God's power' (v. 5).

Paul continues the theme he introduced in 1 Corinthians 1. He reminds the Corinthian Christians how he came to them initially. He came timidly, in weakness and apprehensively. He brought them the mystery of the gospel in simple words, and with only one purpose, to tell them of Christ and the cross.

We wonder if this approach was in part because of where he had been just prior to Corinth: Athens. There, in the meeting of the Athenian Council, he'd spoken to other Greeks who valued rhetoric and clever words. Tolerantly, they'd given him a hearing. He'd tried to connect with them philosophically. Although they'd listened, they were not inclined to believe what he preached.

Since only a few in Athens believed the gospel, perhaps Paul had rethought his approach and decided to stick to the basics. His fear and trembling may have been that of one who is prepared but apprehensive about his delivery or reception. It's the one who although unprepared is cocky and nonchalant who needs to beware of where overconfidence and pride lead.

Happily in Corinth the Holy Spirit confirmed his message irrefutably. Things started to happen. People believed the gospel and, in the midst of a polluted society, lives were cleansed and plainly changed. Changed lives speak for themselves eloquently without flowery resumés.

A few years ago God used the film, *The Passion of the Christ*, to focus people on the person and purpose of Christ. The Barna Group, which surveyed 1,600 American adults about the film, said: 'In a society that revolves around relativism, spiritual diversity, tolerance and independence, galvanising such intense consideration of Jesus Christ is a major achievement in itself.'

Millions of people said they'd altered some pre-existing belief or behaviour because of the film's message. A television documentary and a book, *Changed Lives: Miracles of the Passion*, detailing some of the changes the film brought about, followed. The documentary's producer said the movie was only a vehicle; it was God who changed lives. Paul would heartily agree.

Truly Blessed

'Blessed are the people whose God is the LORD' (v. 15).

Psalm 144 is ascribed to David, possibly because some of its verses parallel verses of Psalms 8 and 18, which were written by him. From the start the psalmist salutes God as his rock, strength, military instructor, his goodness, fortress, high tower, deliverer, shield, object of his trust and the one who brings his people into line.

These expressions fit the experience of one who faced conflicts in a challenging terrain. We can also find their applications to readiness for the spiritual warfare Paul writes about in 2 Corinthians 10 and Ephesians 6.

The psalmist sandwiches humankind's weakness and transience – as frail and fleeting as a shadow or breath – between God's might and power, displayed in nature. When the psalmist speaks of our helplessness in this context, especially in the face of those who would harm us, he underlines our need for a divine deliverer.

Since the writer is confident in God's ability to bring victory, he says he'll sing a new song of praise to God in anticipation of deliverance and the attending blessings of a peaceful society where youth live to maturity, where there is plenty of work and food, where people are prosperous enough to be generous and where no hostilities threaten the public.

That Old Testament image of the ideal civilisation would even today be more than many countries know or could envisage. But temporal success is not necessarily evidence of God's blessing.

More important than privileged circumstances and a stable society, as wonderful as these underserved delights may be, are the blessings of belonging to the living God. Paul writes: 'Praise be to the God and Father of our Lord Jesus Christ, who has blessed us in the heavenly realms with every spiritual blessing in Christ' (Ephesians 1:3).

Then whatever our earthly situation, in spite of, not because of temporal prosperity, we can say, 'How blessed the people who have GOD for God!' (Psalm 144:15, *MSG*).

Open Secret

'We speak of God's secret wisdom, a wisdom that has been hidden and that God destined for our glory before time began' (v. 7).

A child who knows how to add or subtract has learned some mathematical basics. The high-school student who works out an algebraic formula can solve a complex equation because he's learned more principles, properties, symbols and functions. Yet he still employs basic mathematical methods. New knowledge doesn't displace old knowledge, it builds on it.

Although Paul didn't claim to come to the Corinthians with the type of wisdom their world prized, he wasn't a proponent of ignorance either. He announced the gospel to those who hadn't heard it in basic terms and explained in detail what living out the gospel meant for those maturing in the faith.

As people move into different stages of maturity, their understanding grows. Although spiritual wisdom is something like the ageing process or the mathematical learning process, it has the unique dynamic of the Spirit of God about it. Since only God's Spirit knows the mind of God, only he can reveal to us the things of God. Spiritually minded people grasp spiritual truths more readily.

The wisdom of God that Paul writes about is a mystery, an open secret understandable by any who have purposed in their hearts to walk with God in obedience and are maturing in the faith. They are sensitive to and guided by the Spirit. These are those Paul calls spiritual people.

Our spiritual discoveries are not so much *ours* as they are the Spirit of God's revelations to us. Not that the process is automatic. We are still involved in studying the Bible and listening for what the Spirit highlights for our hearts to ponder, to believe, to act upon.

God's wisdom is something mysterious that goes deep into the interior of his purposes. You don't find it lying around on the surface. It's not the latest message, but more like the oldest – what God determined as the way to bring out his best in us, long before we ever arrived on the scene. (v. 7, *MSG*)

A Mature Diet

'Anyone who lives on milk, being still an infant, is not acquainted with the teaching about righteousness. But solid food is for the mature, who by constant use have trained themselves to distinguish good from evil'
(Hebrews 5:13, 14).

In 1 Corinthians 3 Paul continues his discourse about the importance of becoming spiritually minded people. His plain analogy about giving them milk when they were infants in the faith is clear. He laments that some have stayed exclusively on milk far too long. Pastors are still frustrated to have grey-haired babies who want to be coddled.

What has Paul noticed that makes him take the Corinthians to task for their lack of maturity in Christ, their lack of discernment? Most translations use the words envy, strife and division in verse 3, meaning they were off the mark in thought, word and deed.

Mentally they harboured grudges and hostile attitudes to others. Verbally they were contentious and tried to prove themselves or their faction superior. In actions they separated themselves into parties. Misguided thoughts led to evil speaking which led to splitting up. So Paul called them 'still worldly'. The Corinthians' behaviour probably resembled that of their unregenerate society, but that did not excuse them.

Beyond salvation, they didn't understand how the message of Christ crucified applied to their lives. Paul wanted to move them forward to sanctified living which would be evident in Christlike attitudes and actions.

Since they misunderstood the message of the cross, they misunderstood the ministry of the Church. The leaders they'd known were sent to help them mature in Christ. It wasn't a contest. Apollos and Paul weren't in competition for rewards. They were on the same team. If they were faithful to the task God gave them, he would reward them. Besides, they were just instruments God used, only God could bring people to new life.

It's easier to see immaturity in others than in ourselves. Through today's Scripture, does the Lord hold a mirror to our souls? If so, what does he ask of us? Only he can change our hearts and make us sensitive to his direction and will, but we need to ask him to do so.

God's Builders

'If what he has built survives, he will receive his reward' (v. 14).

On his journeys Paul would have seen many examples of construction of all types, sizes and stages of completion. He observed what the process entailed in effort and time. He could have thought of the temple in Jerusalem, a house on Straight Street in Damascus, synagogues, pagan temples, houses where he stayed on his journeys, a jail in Philippi. Even his own experience with tent-making may have given him an appreciation for the complexities of building more permanent structures.

In describing his ministry role, Paul shifts from the metaphor of a gardener planting seeds to a builder laying foundations. Paul's readers simply had to look around them for illustrations of projects.

The city of Corinth was razed by the Romans in 146 BC. About 100 years later Julius Caesar's building boom re-established the commercial metropolis when he made it the capital of a Roman province, so they were surrounded by great buildings.

Paul didn't waste time experimenting with variations, but laid the foundation he was sure about. He gave the facts of the gospel and offered salvation through the cross of Christ. He didn't usually spend enough time in a single place to do much more. Since it was a good foundation, others could build on it confidently.

Some would build with enduring values in view. They would teach sound doctrine with worthy motives. Yet some would unwisely not take care in how they built and could get things off-balance or below standard. Paul may have had a particular Corinthian church leader in mind or perhaps he meant that each believer has a choice in how he builds his life in Christ.

Paul knew that at the end of the day, Christ's return would reveal who lived and built for the King. We pray with songwriter Albert Orsborn that God would cleanse us, use us and keep us living for him:

> All my work is for the Master,
> He is all my heart's desire;
> O that he may count me faithful
> In the day that tries by fire!
> (*SASB* 522)

The Church is God's Temple

'You are of Christ, and Christ is of God' (v. 23).

In verse 16 for the first of ten times in 1 Corinthians, Paul introduces an undeniable statement with, 'Don't you know?' Here he continues: 'that all of you together are the temple of God and that the Spirit of God lives in you?' (*NLT*). We're told that in this instance the word 'you' is plural and means the church, not individuals.

Paul continues the building metaphor. In the first century Christians mainly met for worship and instruction in their homes. Although most Corinthian believers probably would not have seen the temple in Jerusalem, they could still relate to the concept of a building dedicated to divinity. The handful of Jewish believers in their midst would be acquainted with what Scripture said about the tabernacle and the temple.

Paul had seen more than one type of temple on his journeys. Further, as a Jewish scholar he would have been familiar with the history of the temple in Jerusalem. He would have understood its significance and spiritual symbolism. But he didn't burden his readers with those details.

They were the temple of God because God's Spirit lived in the church. Allowing divisions and dissension was serious since it tore down the church. Recent history of their city could remind them of what razed buildings looked like. Divisions split the church into disconnected ruins and obstructed the work of the Spirit.

The worship of intelligence and worldly wisdom, prevalent in Greek society of the day, had crept into the church and was the basis of divisive party preference. Paul addresses intellectual pride that leads to a judgmental and elitist spirit in leaders and followers. He suggests that those who think they're wise by worldly standards are 'fools'. It reminds us of when Jesus heard the disciples' dispute over who was greatest, and turned their attention to the kingdom value of childlikeness.

So, enough of prizing human wisdom over God's, enough of dissension and division, says Paul. Remember you are meant for a much bigger outlook than that, you are Christ's! Now as God's Church, think and act that way.

ACTS 17:22–28

World Day of Prayer

'The God who made the world and everything in it is the Lord of heaven and earth and does not live in temples built by hands. And he is not served by human hands, as if he needed anything, because he himself gives all men life and breath and everything else' (vv. 24, 25).

Today is World Day of Prayer. As the day began at dawn in the Pacific Ocean and as it continues across continents until the last services are held in Samoa, the world is encircled by thirty-six hours of prayer.

Every four years an international committee chooses the themes and countries that will prepare a suggested order of service for use around the world. In addition to what that country contributes on the theme, everyone is asked to pray for the country itself. Participation in a World Day of Prayer service helps us to understand Christians of other cultures, their needs and how they comprehend the biblical passage in their context.

Christians in Cameroon have prepared the focus for the gatherings to be held around the world today. Their theme is from Psalm 150, 'Let Everything That Has Breath Praise God'.

When Paul spoke to the council of the curious in Athens, just prior to his first visit to Corinth, he told them that the Creator of all gave humankind everything – including our very breath. He knew that the Old Testament says God gave all living creatures the breath of life, but humans particularly. He could have reflected on Ezekiel's experience in the valley of bones when God revitalised dry bones and gave them breath, life.

So we think of the people of Cameroon today, the land which Portuguese explorers in the 1400s named *Camarões* or River of Prawns because of the abundance of those creatures. The African nation is comparable in size to Papua New Guinea (last year's focus of the World Day of Prayer). As we learn more about them, we pray for the needs of the people in Cameroon.

To pray:

Lord, please keep us alert to the burdens of the Church. We also ask to become more aware of the rich faith and contributions of fellow Christians around the world.

Leave Judgment to God

'Therefore judge nothing before the appointed time; wait till the Lord comes. He will bring to light what is hidden in darkness and will expose the motives of men's hearts. At that time each will receive his praise from God' (v. 5).

Paul continues on the subject of misplaced loyalties that he wrote about in 1 Corinthians 3. The prominent men behind whom the Corinthians lined up aren't party leaders as such. In fact Paul says they should think of him and Apollos and Peter as servants and stewards of God.

The word he uses for servants means 'rowers', but not the type who take part in an annual regatta. These rowers are on the lowest tier of the triple-decked galley ships that used slaves to propel them.

They're stewards or household managers, in charge of a great deal, but still themselves in the service of a master. They're assigned great tasks and given much freedom, but they have to be utterly reliable in what they do and accountable to their master. As such God will be their judge, not the Corinthians.

Paul says we make judgments about each other, and some of these assessments may be quite true. We also judge ourselves, sometimes too harshly or too leniently as we cope with what we know of ourselves and what we choose. Yet that shouldn't be the basis of what motivates our conduct. The judgment that matters most and is most accurate yet merciful is God's. Only he knows all the circumstances and true motives.

The Corinthians had been judging each other and usurping God's prerogative. They were to leave this to God to sort out at the second coming and final judgment. It's his judgment that ultimately matters.

———

To pray:

Search me, O God, and know my heart today;
Try me, O Saviour, know my thoughts, I pray;
See if there be some wicked way in me;
Cleanse me from every sin, and set me free.

Edwin Orr [11]

Echoes from a Cave

'I cry out, GOD, call out: "You're my last chance, my only hope for life!"'
(v. 5, MSG).

In some translations the heading of Psalm 142 makes reference to a cave. This may have been at En Gedi (meaning 'the spring of the kid'), an oasis along the western shores of the Dead Sea containing a rare freshwater spring. En Gedi was part of the allotment of land given to the tribe of Judah (Joshua 15). The cave was where David took refuge from King Saul around 1000 BC.

Temporarily living in a cave would give anyone pause for thought. Was it dark, damp, temperate? Did it seem like a womb or a tomb? In verses 1 and 2 David may address others who were with him. The verses also set the stage. David intends to cry out loud for mercy and in full disclosure of his trouble. But he directs the rest of the psalm to God. Read his prayer aloud.

David admits his desperation. He claims that no one stands with him to help protect him, and he sees no safe way out (v. 4). His life is at stake and he feels helpless if not depressed (v. 6). Our situation may not be as intense, but life brings all of us times of extremity, often through no fault of our own. Whether or not we're adept at coping with trouble, we all need some help outside of ourselves. Those who admit it are wise.

Almost simultaneously with bemoaning his plight, David acknowledges that God is his only hope. He remembers that in the past when he was overwhelmed, God knew his path (v. 3). That recollection emboldens him to cry for help. He doesn't barter with God, but says that divine deliverance will give him new opportunity to praise God's name publicly. He's sure that his prayer is heard and that the righteous will join him in rejoicing at God's bountiful dealings.

To ponder:

How does time in a 'cave' change the focus and concentration of your prayer? When God answers that prayer, how do you give others opportunity to join in your joy?

Humility, a Plus or Minus?

'When we are cursed, we bless; when we are persecuted, we endure it; when we are slandered, we answer kindly' (vv. 12, 13).

To make a film in Mumbai, India, where most male actors are well-built, a director said he had to search elsewhere for someone slight enough to lend the 'loser' aspect that his main character required. Many cultures prefer leaders who exhibit physical strength, assertiveness, self-confidence and certainty. Humility may look as much like weakness as a bony build.

Since Greeks believed Plato's teaching that humility was shameful, the trait of a slave, a sign of weakness, it was difficult for Paul to advocate humility. But Paul reminds his readers that just as he and Apollos hold a humble perspective of themselves and each other, they should too. Paul warns them not to go beyond what is written. God's word elevates God, not people. Abiding by it would help them not to inflate one leader and deflate another.

Paul asks three pointed questions to shock the pride of the Corinthians. Who gives you the right to discriminate against leaders? What do you have that wasn't given to you? Why do you act as if you generated what only God can give?

Those who are self-satisfied and spiritually satiated when there's always more to learn, fool themselves. In contrast with the Corinthians' pride, Paul says apostles should exhibit humility.

While the Corinthians think themselves wise, strong and honourable, the apostles are thought fools, weak and despised. The way they're treated is like the way a conquering general parades his captives through the streets on their way to the arena to die.

The specifics Paul gives about what apostles endure and how they respond would have bewildered his readers. Why would anyone bear such abuse and then, instead of retaliating, bless their offenders? The philosopher Aristotle had taught the virtue of refusing to tolerate insults. In contrast, Paul presents the implications of the message of the cross.

Christ our King, now exalted by God, first humbled himself and was obedient to death on the cross. We can't improve on, reverse or replace his pattern, however uncomfortable it makes us.

A Fatherly Reminder

'So how should I prepare to come to you? As a severe disciplinarian who makes you toe the mark? Or as a good friend and counsellor who wants to share heart-to-heart with you? You decide' (v. 21, MSG).

Paul concludes the section of the letter dealing with division and dissension by appealing to the Corinthian believers as their spiritual father. They had many church leaders now, but only he could claim to have initially brought them to new life in Christ. Their welfare was his serious concern. As was the case in society then, and still is in many places now, the father was the one who was legally responsible for the family. He could delegate, but the final duty was his.

In a later letter Paul would write specifically to parents and children and remind fathers to nourish their children in the instruction and admonition of the Lord (Ephesians 6:4). Here he uses the same words when he says he writes sternly not to shame but to warn them. He wants them to take his rebuke as a kindness (in the spirit of Psalm 141:5).

Paul wants his unruly children to straighten up for their own good. His fatherly appeal to them is from his great affection for them as well as from their indebtedness to him for bringing them the gospel. He asks them to imitate him in the faith.

Then he promises the next best thing to a visit from him. He'll send Timothy. They would remember him from Paul's initial visit. Besides being Paul's co-worker, he was like a son to Paul and, by extension, their brother. Timothy could personally remind them of Paul's life in Christ. He could verify that Paul's living and teachings were consistent, and theirs should be as well.

Some in Corinth might shrug off Paul's warnings, but when the time was right the apostle would visit them himself. Then he would see who was simply full of talk and who was empowered by God. It was up to them whether he would still need to confront and discipline them or whether he could enjoy heart-to-heart fellowship when he came.

———

To ponder:

Is my Christian living consistent? Could I use a reminder to live more fully aware of the presence of Christ?

Spring Cleaning

'For Christ, our Passover lamb, has been sacrificed. Therefore let us keep the Festival, not with the old yeast, the yeast of malice and wickedness, but with bread without yeast, the bread of sincerity and truth' (vv. 7, 8).

In the area of New York where I live, many Jews strictly observe their holidays, including Passover in the spring (this year 30 March to 6 April). Preparation includes extensive cleaning, especially of the kitchen, and removal of all chametz which means far more than just leavening agents. Even the diet of pets is affected. The usual cooking pots, utensils and dishes can't be used. Stoves and ovens are thoroughly cleaned, then after twenty-four hours they are set on 'high' to burn off anything that may have been missed.

In 1 Corinthians 5, Paul uses the illustration of scouring the house at Passover to be sure all the leaven is expunged. Likewise the Church, in reverence for Christ, our Passover sacrifice, should be motivated to be free from all known sin. Paul speaks to church discipline on specific issues.

He may have been shocked at certain reported sins, but was just as stunned that the church hadn't been heart-broken over them and dealt with them. He doesn't excuse the Corinthians because they live in a corrupt culture. Neither does he promote a monastic life. But he wants to protect them from the callousness to which condoning sin could lead.

In particular he warns of lax morality, greed and idolatry. Applied individually, these are sins against ourselves, our neighbours and God. They are exactly the opposite of what Jesus said were the greatest commandments.

'The most important one,' answered Jesus, 'is this: "Hear, O Israel, the Lord our God, the Lord is one. Love the Lord your God with all your heart and with all your soul and with all your mind and with all your strength." The second is this: "Love your neighbour as yourself." There is no commandment greater than these' (Mark 12:29–32).

To pray:

Holy Spirit, I want to love God supremely. Cleanse me from all sin. Help me to genuinely seek and do the right today.

Judge for Yourself

'The day is coming when the world is going to stand before a jury made up of Christians. If someday you are going to rule on the world's fate, wouldn't it be a good idea to practice on some of these smaller cases?' (v. 2, MSG)

Many television dramas involve courtroom scenes which give the viewer fictionalised glimpses of the legal system. In the USA there is a network dedicated to syndicated programmes of arbitration cases usually presided over by a colourful judge. On occasion, portions of high-profile criminal cases have been televised.

Legal battles can be fascinating to spectators. Although educational, it is less glamorous to receive a jury summons, join the jury pool and wait through the many lengthy steps of selection, arguments and deliberation.

In Paul's day, Greeks were litigious and found courtrooms entertaining. Some cases involved hundreds on their juries. It was a civic duty that took up much of an average citizen's time. Regarding taking each other to court, Paul writes primarily to Greeks at Corinth. Jews were not in the habit of going to court against each other.

As a Jew, Paul found the Corinthians' rush to bring legal charges against fellow believers appalling. He questioned why believers should look for justice among unbelievers. Weren't there people in the church who could handle internal disputes? Didn't they know that God's people would one day help judge the world? Didn't they know that the unrighteous to whom they turned would not inherit the kingdom?

He catalogues many of the vices rife in their surroundings and reminds them how decadent some of them had been before the Holy Spirit washed, sanctified and justified them in the name of Jesus Christ.

Now they were changed, as different as midday is from midnight. Surely such power could help them work out their internal disputes as well. If we ask for his wisdom, God will give us discernment and help us see things his way, righteously and justly. With Abraham we confidently declare: 'Will not the Judge of all the earth do right?' (Genesis 18:25).

Free not to Sin

*'You are not your own; you were bought at a price. Therefore honour
God with your body' (vv. 19, 20).*

Paul turns from talking about disputes and courtrooms but stays with
the theme of what is lawful. The Corinthians were struggling with the
implications of freedom from Old Testament law. Paul speaks to the limits
of liberty here as he will in more detail later.

He flings out three of their own sayings and then counters them. First:
'Everything is permissible for me' (v. 12). Although theoretically true, Paul
reminds them that liberty needs to be qualified with the principle of love
concerning both others and ourselves. Liberty that damages someone else
doesn't love. Liberty that enslaves us is a contradiction.

Next: 'Food for the stomach and the stomach for food' (v. 13). This
saying reminds us of 'We eat to live and live to eat'. Although we smile, it
sounds hedonistic, especially when we extend the idea to other physical
pleasures. Paul counters that a person is not compartmentalised. Christ's
resurrection shows that. What we do with our bodies affects our spirits. We
are meant for union with the Lord.

Finally: 'All other sins a man commits are outside his body' (v. 18). Paul
denies this directly with his comeback that sexual sin is against one's own
body. And if that were not enough, Paul indicates that sexual sin grieves the
indwelling Holy Spirit as well as God the Father who bought us with the
price of the death of his Son.

Seen in that light, Christian liberty is a serious matter. We are not our
own. Our 'rights' are less important than our 'oughts' to our Saviour.
Wrote Daniel Webster Whittle:

> Not my own, but saved by Jesus,
> Who redeemed me by his blood;
> Gladly I accept the message,
> I belong to Christ the Lord.
> *(SASB 514)*

To ponder:

**How have I experienced God's forgiveness and deep cleansing? Do I also ask for
his pre-emptive aid?**

Wed or Not

'Each man must love his wife as he loves himself' (Ephesians 5:33, NLT).

Gnosticism, which was prevalent in Greek culture in the first century, taught that human beings were divine souls trapped in a material world made by an imperfect god. No doubt this philosophy influenced the Corinthian believers.

When some people have chronic illness and long to be free from the body, they want to believe the ancient idea that the body is unimportant or evil. For others, discounting the body and what they do in the flesh is a way of rationalising immoral behaviour. Looking down on the body can be taken to another extreme which promotes asceticism.

In all cases we need to be reminded that God created us as triune persons with body, mind and spirit and that all parts matter to him and should to us.

In 1 Corinthians 7, Paul addresses some issues that the Corinthians had raised in a letter to him. We need to remember that they lived in an extremely morally polluted culture. It's also helpful to keep in mind that Paul thought the second coming of Christ was imminent. In that context, his advice would be strict and temporary.

They asked if they should avoid marriage. Paul says, considering their society, marriage was preferable. They asked if they should abstain from sex in marriage. Paul says marriage is a partnership. Any period of abstinence should be a mutual decision, brief and with a spiritual purpose.

Paul does not have a low view of marriage. He uses it in Ephesians as an illustration of Christ and the Church. Here he recommends the widowed or unmarried (he was probably one of these) to stay that way and the married to stay that way. Any remarriage should be to a believer.

William Barclay sums up the chapter:

No man should be ashamed of the body God gave him, the heart God put into him, the instincts that, by God's creation dwell within him. Christianity will teach him, not how to eliminate them, but how to use them in such a way that passion is pure and human love the most ennobling thing in all God's world.[12]

Fragrant and Salted

'May my prayer be set before you like incense; may the lifting up of my hands be like the evening sacrifice' (v. 2).

For most people, a smell can trigger recollections of their earliest memories – meat roasting, damp ashes after a fire, a cleaning product, the scent of spring flowers or summer rain. Some children's books use scratch and sniff pages to enhance the story.

There are people employed to use their keen sense of smell – in perfumeries for instance. They can discriminate between slight variations of fragrance. Those with allergies learn to avoid particular scent triggers. Most of us just know if a scent is pleasant or not.

For some Christians, worship services include the regular use of incense. It's a reminder of the Old Testament's requisite incense made exclusively for sacred service and burned daily in the tabernacle, then in the temple. Exodus 30 says it was to be made of four specific fragrant spices and salt.

In the New Testament, Zechariah was on special assignment in the temple representing the people to God. While the people prayed outside at the hour of incense or prayer, he attended to the incense which symbolised the prayers of the nation. As he ministered, surrounded by a unique aroma, the angel Gabriel appeared with God's message that Zechariah and Elizabeth would have a divinely appointed son, John.

In today's psalm, David asks that his prayer be placed before the Lord like the special incense. In the same verse he asks that his worship would be seen as the evening sacrifice. The word he uses for sacrifice is *minchah*, likely the thank-offering consisting of grain, oil, incense and salt. Perhaps the salt used in both the incense and the *minchah* signified purity, incorruptibility or covenant.

In Revelation 5 and 8 we see believers' prayers paired with fragrant incense in heaven. Of the sacrifices we can offer God, perhaps sincere prayer is one that can most be considered 'as an aroma pleasing to the Lord'.

———

To pray:

Lord, remind me by any means to daily offer you an aroma that pleases you, I mean my honest prayer.

The Cross is Made to My Measure

Our guest writer for the next three weeks (other than Sundays 21 and 28 March) is Commissioner Makoto Yoshida. A Salvation Army officer for more than forty years, he has been a corps officer (church minister), training college officer, divisional commander and staff officer at Territorial Headquarters in Tokyo. At International Headquarters, London, he was International Secretary for the South Pacific and East Asia Zone. He is now Territorial Commander for Japan. He has been married to Karou for thirty-six years and the commissioners have two sons and a daughter. Commissioner Yoshida writes:

One of my favourite books is *Prayers of Life*[13] by Michel Quoist. I first met this book when I was training to be an officer. Prayers in this book were not the 'how to pray' type, but the deeply heartfelt prayers of the writer. I was able to identify with many of them personally.

One of the prayers is 'Jesus is nailed to the cross' in which the writer prays:

> Lord, you stretch at full length on the cross.
>> There.
>> Without a doubt, it is made for you.
>> Thus, Lord, I must gather my body, my heart, my spirit,
> And stretch myself at full length on the cross of the present
> Moment.
> The cross is ready, to my measure.
>> You present it to me each day, each minute,
>> and I must lie on it.

As we ponder the happenings of our Lord on the way to Jerusalem and at his crucifixion, may we be able to see the cross which is made to measure for each of us.

> Take up thy cross and follow me,
> I hear the blessed Saviour call;
> How can I make a lesser sacrifice
> When Jesus gave his all?
> *Alfred Henry Ackley* (*SASB* [American edition] 978)

The Cross Reveals Our Sins . . .

In the Pharisees

' "*Woe to you, teachers of the law and Pharisees, you hypocrites!
You clean the outside of the cup and dish, but inside they are full
of greed and self-indulgence*" ' (v. 25).

Today and for the next few days we will be looking at the message of the
cross. The cross tells us of our sins. We can see them in those who were
at the cross when the Lord was crucified.

There were several groups of people surrounding the cross. They
included the Pharisees, teachers of the law. We see sins in them. They are
clearly found in Matthew 23. They were directly responsible for putting
Jesus on the cross.

They kept trying to find chances to kill Jesus: 'The chief priests, the
teachers of the law and the leaders among the people were trying to kill
him' (Luke 19:47). Their desire to kill Jesus was an outward sign of their
inward sin. The great sin in their heart was human pride, which did not
allow them to admit their sin and instead led them to put themselves in the
place of God.

Is not their sin our sin as well? We put ourselves in the centre. Even
when we say we serve God, we sometimes tell God to use us in the way *we*
want to be used. Do we not place something other than God in his place –
our education, qualifications, experiences, achievements, wealth or
reputation? Do we not see ourselves as better than others? Do we not feel
important when we achieve something and someone compliments us?

It is easier to see other people's sins and mistakes than it is to see our
own. Unconsciously we are often blind to our own faults, just as the
Pharisees were. We too put Jesus on the cross.

———

To pray:

**Lord, help us to see our true selves in your eyes and to recognise our sin – the
sin of putting something other than you in your place.**

The Cross Reveals our Sins . . .

In the Crowd

' "Why? What crime has he committed?" asked Pilate. But they shouted all the louder, "Crucify him!" ' (v. 23).

Those at the cross included a crowd of people who only a few days before welcomed Jesus, shouting: 'Hosanna! Blessed is he who comes in the name of the Lord! Blessed is the coming kingdom of our father David! Hosanna in the highest!' (Mark 11:9, 10). Now, this same crowd are shouting, 'Crucify him!' Even allowing for the influence of the chief priests who are stirring them up to have Pilate release Barabbas instead, it is a surprising change of mood.

What made them change so much? Perhaps they were disappointed when they realised that the coming kingdom of 'their father David' was not what they expected. Their expectation was for a worldly kingdom, not a spiritual one. They did not understand the symbolic meaning of Jesus entering Jerusalem on an ass, a sign of peace.

Or perhaps they found it too hard to be different from the rest. Perhaps some were reluctant to cry 'Crucify him!' but could not bring themselves to stand out from the mob. Again we see their sins reflected in ourselves. In non-Christian countries, particularly, it is not easy to be a Christian among people who have a different belief or no belief at all. We do not want to be different from others. We do not want to be seen as strange.

This is especially true in Eastern cultures. In Japan, when Salvationists are collecting donations door-to-door for The Salvation Army's work they are often asked, 'How much did other people give you?' The question reveals the human tendency to want to be seen to be like others. When Peter denied Jesus he might have been afraid to be different from the others around him. If we were in the crowd at the foot of the cross, what would we have shouted – 'Crucify him!' or 'Hosanna in the highest!'?

———

Prayer topic:

Christians who need courage to be different in a non-Christian society.

The Cross Reveals our Sins . . .

In the Disciples

'Then all the disciples deserted him and fled' (v. 56).

In Gethsemane, when Jesus was arrested all the disciples deserted him. Soon Peter was to deny Jesus three times. We are not sure how many of the disciples were at the cross; perhaps some watched from a distance with a feeling of utter hopelessness.

The twelve had been chosen by Jesus and for three years had been taught about the kingdom that was to come. Yet they had not understood the true meaning of what Jesus had said. Peter said to Jesus, 'We have left everything to follow you! What then will there be for us?' (19:27). They boasted that they would follow Jesus even to death, yet they deserted Jesus when they were most needed.

So the disciples, too, were among those who put Jesus on the cross. But how can we blame them? We are, or could be, the same as them. We may not desert Jesus literally; we may still attend church and support Christian activities and contribute to its work financially. But there are ways to 'desert' Jesus in a spiritual sense.

If we commit sins such as gossip, self-seeking, boasting, dishonesty or back-biting, then we are deserting Jesus, and putting him on the cross. If we are not shining as lights in a dark world we are hiding the Light of the world on the cross.

But when the Holy Spirit came on the day of Pentecost the disciples were filled with the Spirit and became true followers of Jesus. The fruit of the Spirit became evident in them and they became courageous. Until we are filled with the Holy Spirit we will have the same weakness and those fruits will not be seen in us.

The good news is that what happened to the disciples can be our experience too.

To pray:

Lord, fill us with the Holy Sprit so that we can be your true followers.

Counted and Classed Among the Wicked

'He was counted and classed among the wicked
(the outlaws, the criminals)' (v. 37, AB).
'It is written: "And he was numbered with the transgressors";
and I tell you that this must be fulfilled in me' (v. 37).

One of the most famous verses in the Bible must be John 3:16: 'For God so loved the world that he gave his one and only Son.' The core of this is expressed in the words of the apostle Paul: '(Jesus) made himself nothing, taking the very nature of a servant, being made in human likeness. And being found in appearance as a man, he humbled himself' (Philippians 2:7, 8). God became human to identify with us. Or as our songwriter-general, Albert Orsborn, wrote:

> He came right down to me,
> He came right down to me,
> To condescend to be my friend,
> He came right down to me.
> (*SASB* 398)

There is a story in Japan in which a man wants to help his friend in hell by throwing him a spider's thread. If the thread is cut, the man will be safe but his friend will fall down to hell again. This is not what Jesus did to save us. He came right down to us with the risk that he too would die.

Jesus came down not only to be human but 'was numbered with the transgressors. For he bore the sin of many' (Isaiah 53:12). When Jesus referred to that prophecy he continued, 'I tell you that this must be fulfilled in me. Yes, what is written about me is reaching its fulfilment' (Luke 22:37). This is the supreme expression of God's love to us. As songwriter Graham Kendrick writes:

> Such love, pure as the whitest snow;
> Such love, weeps for the shame I know;
> Such love, paying the debt I owe;
> O Jesus, such love.[14]

Those in White Robes

'But God demonstrates his own love for us in this: While we were still sinners, Christ died for us' (v. 8).

We have looked at the Pharisees, the crowd and the disciples. They put Jesus on the cross, but it was for them and for us that Jesus died. If salvation depended upon our righteous deeds, would anyone live lives righteous enough to earn them salvation? The answer must surely be, very few.

'Blessed are they whose transgressions are forgiven, whose sins are covered,' says Paul in Romans 4:7. He does not say the sins have disappeared, he says they are forgiven and 'covered'. God forgives and covers because he loves us. Forgiveness is his prerogative, it comes only through his grace. And here's the truly good news: it's for everyone. 'Whosoever will, may come' is the Bible's message of invitation.

In the book of Revelation John writes: "Then one of the elders asked me, "These in white robes – who are they, and where did they come from?" I answered, "Sir, you know." And he said, "These are they who have come out of the great tribulation; they have washed their robes and made them white in the blood of the Lamb"' (7:13, 14).

The only condition for entry into the kingdom is to be washed by the blood of the Lamb and to be wearing white robes.

In Japan, a former criminal felt so hopeless about his life one freezing cold winter's night that he flung himself into a river, intending to drown himself. But he was swept to the bank. So, instead, he cut his wrist with a piece of broken glass. But still he did not die. Someone took him to a Salvation Army hostel where, counselled by the staff, he found the Lord. If salvation came only from good deeds, he could not have found it, but the grace of God saved him. He is now in white robes washed by the blood of the Lamb.

Each of us, if we wish, can cry out with the multitude: 'Salvation belongs to our God, who sits on the throne, and to the Lamb' (Revelation 7:10).

———

To pray:

Thank you Father, that we can stand among those in white robes, by your grace.

83

Jesus Predicts His Death

'He then began to teach them that the Son of Man must suffer many things and be rejected . . . and that he must be killed and after three days rise again' (v. 31).

We now look at some incidents in Mark's Gospel that happened to Jesus on his way to Jerusalem. During this period Jesus predicts three times that he is going to be crucified and resurrected (8:31; 9:31; 10:33).

On the first and third occasions, immediately after his predictions, Jesus spoke to his disciples about following him: 'If anyone would come after me, he must deny himself and take up his cross and follow me' (8:34). Later he asks: 'Can you drink the cup I drink or be baptised with the baptism I am baptised with?'(10:38).

Jesus clearly felt it was vital that his disciples understood why he came to earth. They had to understand that he came to die, and that to follow him means we too must be prepared to die. So he connects following him with death on the cross. But the disciples, at this stage at least, cannot understand.

By the time Mark wrote his Gospel, the cross had become linked to the resurrection. We now know the cross leads to new life in Christ, as Paul declares: 'Now if we died with Christ, we believe that we will also live with him' (Romans 6:8). Dying must precede rising. As resurrection followed Christ's cross, new life follows our dying to ourselves.

When Gospel-writer Luke records what Jesus said about taking up the cross, he adds the word 'daily' and says, 'he must deny himself and take up his cross *daily* and follow me' (Luke 9:23). We see here that dying to self is not a one-time incident. Martin Luther said our lives are a continual repentance. He surely had in mind the concept of our need for daily dying as the key to daily victorious living.

Weaponry and Words

*'I know that the LORD secures justice for the poor and upholds
the cause of the needy' (v. 12).*

Psalms 140–143 deal with similar topics. In them David confidently
seeks God's deliverance from sinful and violent people who seek to
harm him. When he writes of evil men in verses 1 and 2 of Psalm 140, the
psalmist probably thinks of King Saul and his co-conspirators against
David's life. They act like cunning serpents, full of venom. Some of their
honed weapons are their words.

Even well-meaning words can wound; how much more so intentional
slander! More than one thoughtless or arrogant word from a forked tongue
has wounded a fragile spirit or discouraged a young or harried believer.

On a tour of Berg Eltz, a well-preserved castle near the Moselle River in
Germany, I viewed a cross-section of its eight-hundred-year history.
Besides the rooms designed for various functions of daily life, its double-
storeyed entrance room-turned-arsenal displayed an array of jousting
lances, halberds, fifteenth-century wall-rifles, fourteenth-century canon-
bolts and weaponry taken as booty from Turkish wars.

Weapons are used to subdue or defend. Spiritual weapons are
formidable too. We think of Paul's admonition to prepare for spiritual battle
with adequate armour. Perhaps he was thinking of the weapons of words
when he wrote, 'Take up the shield of faith, with which you can extinguish
all the flaming arrows of the evil one' (Ephesians 6:16).

David asks that the words the wicked hurl at him would boomerang
back on them. He wants God to catch evildoers in their own traps. Various
versions call the one the psalmist writes about in verse 11 a loudmouth,
slanderer, man of tongue, liar, evil speaker. David asks that this type of
person as well as the violent be unmasked and hunted down. He must have
been personally acquainted with the damage both can do.

Yet he also knows that God brings justice for those who depend on him.
In the end the upright win. God delivers them from the wicked, their
weaponry and their words. We live to praise him. Wherever we are in the
battle today, let's be sure we're helping the cause of our King and trusting
him to defend us even from words.

Like a Little Child

' *"Anyone who will not receive the kingdom of God like a little child will never enter it"* ' (v. 15).

Here is another topic Jesus discussed with his disciples on the way to Jerusalem. He taught them that to enter the kingdom of God they need to become like a little child. What did Jesus mean by this? To become like a little child is to have some of a child's characteristics: simplicity, vulnerability, helplessness.

To say we need a simple faith like a child's does not mean what we believe is simple and superficial. It means 'simple faith in the profound truth'. A little child may say, 'I believe it because my teacher said so'; similarly we may need to say, 'I believe it because it is written in the Bible.' This is the simplicity we are talking about and the deep truth in the Bible is revealed to us by the Holy Spirit's guidance.

What about the helplessness of a little child? We all know a baby is weak and helpless. Only when we become aware of our own helplessness can we totally rely on God. In his letter to the Romans, Paul says: 'Now if I do what I do not want to do, it is no longer I who do it, but it is sin living in me that does it' (7:20).

The first step of the 'Twelve Steps' of Alcoholics Anonymous states: 'We admitted we were powerless over alcohol – that our lives had become unmanageable.' Here we see a similar thinking. Paul is talking about his helplessness toward his sin. Only when we realise our helplessness do we ask God for salvation which he alone can give. No human effort can give us salvation from sin.

There is another point in childlikeness. In Mark 9, Jesus tells his disciples that to welcome a little child in his name is to welcome him. These words come after the disciples dispute among themselves who is the greatest. People often prefer to be friends with a great or famous person rather than an unimportant or poor one. But Jesus tells us to accept a little child.

Human greatness means nothing when we seek salvation from God. Salvation comes only through the cross of Jesus in which we are expected to put simple faith.

One Thing You Lack

'Jesus looked at him and loved him. "One thing you lack," he said. "Go, sell everything you have and give to the poor, and you will have treasure in heaven"' (v. 21).

Mark tells the story of the rich young man straight after the story of little children. It seems intentionally placed. Jesus instructs the young man to sell everything he has. Jesus tells him he must give up all he has been depending upon, so that he may become as dependent as a little child. Perhaps this rich young man had been relying on his great wealth, because he was unwilling to obey and sell everything. As Mark records: 'At this the man's face fell. He went away sad, because he had great wealth' (v. 22).

For us, what holds us back may be our reputation. Or perhaps our prized status in the world. But Jesus says that we can and should depend on only one thing – God alone. Again Jesus tells us to become like a little child who is helpless and weak.

Are we prepared to give up things which are not of God? Sometimes it is more difficult for those who have much to give up what they have. 'How hard it is for the rich to enter the kingdom of God!' (v. 23).

Jesus also tells the young man to give to the poor. In Eastern culture you are expected to give something back when you receive a gift. When you go to someone's wedding you take a gift, but you expect to receive something back from the couple as a 'return gift'. Not to do so would be seen as a discourtesy. However, when you give to the poor you do not expect any return. Giving to the poor is purely and simply caring for the weak without any hope of return.

That is the sort of giving that Christians should engage in.

———————

To pray:

Lord, help me not to depend on anything but you, and to give with no thought of receiving in return.

What Do You Want Me to Do?

' "What do you want me to do for you?" Jesus asked him. The blind man said, "Rabbi, I want to see" ' (v. 51).

Another incident that happens on the way to Jerusalem is the healing of Bartimaeus, the blind man. The key words in this story are the words of Jesus, 'What do you want me to do for you?' The first step for the blind man to get his sight back is to recognise and admit that he is blind. Bartimaeus knows what he really needs is sight, not the money for which he is asking at the roadside.

This applies to our spiritual blindness. Jesus said to the Pharisees, 'If you were blind, you would not be guilty of sin; but now that you claim you can see, your guilt remains' (John 9:41). We may look for things that are not really what we should seek first. We first must know what we really need for our lives. 'Seek first his kingdom and his righteousness' (Matthew 6:33).

The second step is to know who can give sight back and to whom we should turn. Bartimaeus knew it was the Son of David, the Lord Jesus, the one who fulfilled the prophecy: 'He has sent me to proclaim freedom for the prisoners and recovery of sight for the blind' (Luke 4:18).

Bartimaeus was begging for money but when he knew that Jesus of Nazareth was coming, he changed his focus and asked for his sight back. While some other religious people could not admit their blindness and rejected the real life-giver, Bartimaeus was different. Do we know that Jesus can give us sight, spiritual sight, and the real life that we need? Let us be sure we know what we really need and who can give it to us.

Mrs Commissioner Kieko Yamamuro, wife of the first Japanese Salvation Army officer, Commissioner Gunpei Yamamuro, spoke these words on her deathbed: 'God first. Happiness is found only at the foot of the cross.' Are we prepared to say that too?

———

To pray:

Lord, help me to say that I find happiness only in you, you on the cross.

The New Commandment

' "A new command I give you: Love one another. As I have loved you, so you must love one another" ' (v. 34).

Jesus gives his disciples a new command: love one another. For the Jews in the days of Jesus, countless human laws restricted the lives of ordinary people, although they were not always in the authentic spirit of the original God-given law.

Jesus' new commandment is the new way of living. It is not easy to love and accept others. Society seems to reject the weak, while the strong remain dominant. People want to be friends of the famous and the rich rather than the nameless and the poor. Personal benefit and gain tend to come first. But Jesus' command to love one another came new to them.

'One another' is the key concept. It begins with us and our responsibility. Jesus tells us the nature and extent of that love. It's 'as I have loved you'. How did Jesus love? Paul tells us in Romans: 'God demonstrates his own love for us in this: While we were still sinners, Christ died for us' (5:8). It was in Jesus that love was first demonstrated, even before we loved him. Only if we first experience the love of God can we love others in the same manner. In this way we can obey the new commandment.

Shiokari Pass, a novel written by Japanese Christian author Ayako Miura, is based on the true story of a man who sacrificed his life to stop a runaway train. When he knew the train was out of control, he threw himself in front of the train and stopped it. He was a devoted Christian and his action was surely motivated by the sacrificial love of Christ shown to him.

To pray:

Lord, make your love real to us so that we can love one another.

I am the Way

' "I am the way and the truth and the life. No-one comes to the Father except through me" ' (v. 6).

As Jesus approaches the last days before the cross, he must feel it is extremely important to give his disciples some final words, since they will no longer be able to ask him questions or hear his physical voice. He gives them one of the most important truths: he is the only way to God the Father, because in him God revealed his fullness. 'Grace and truth came through Jesus Christ. No-one has ever seen God, but God the One and Only, who is at the Father's side, has made him known' (John 1:17, 18).

Yet the disciples are not satisfied with what Jesus says. Philip wants Jesus to show them the Father (14:8). Jesus answers: 'Believe me when I say that I am in the Father and the Father is in me; or at least believe on the evidence of the miracles themselves' (14:11). Or as Eugene Peterson puts the end of that verse: 'If you can't believe that, believe what you see – these works' (*MSG*).

I know a young man who was brought up by minister parents. He saw something miraculous in his parents' ministry: men becoming changed, people accepting Jesus as their Saviour, the needy being helped in many ways; but he never recognised the signs of God's works in them. However, later when he became aware of God, his spiritual eyes were opened to see God's signs. He now knows that Jesus is the way and is walking in this way.

In the story of Jesus changing water to wine, his first miracle, his disciples started to put their faith in him (John 2:11) but we know that not all who were there saw the miracle as a sign that Jesus was the way. There are many signs around us which show that Jesus is the way to God, yet sometimes we are slow to see them.

———

To pray:

Father, open our eyes to see what you are doing in our world. Then help us to realise and affirm that Jesus is the only way to come to you.

A Man on an Ass

*'If anyone asks you, "Why are you doing this?" tell him, "The Lord
needs it and will send it back here shortly"' (v. 3).*

On the day when Jesus entered Jerusalem for the last time, people
welcomed him shouting, 'Hosanna! Blessed is he who comes in the
name of the Lord! Blessed is the coming kingdom of our father David!
Hosanna in the highest!' (11:9, 10). But there was a big gap between
what the people expected from the coming king and the real King, Jesus
on an ass.

The prophets of old spoke of Jesus so beautifully and made people
expect a kind of king that the people hoped for. We wonder what the people
thought when they saw Jesus on an ass. They are the same crowd who
would shout 'Crucify him!' only a few days later.

We too confess that Jesus is Lord and say God is first and everything
belongs to him. Yet when we really look at ourselves we have to admit that
sometimes we do not put Jesus first. Instead we make excuses for not doing
so. For example, when we are financially constrained, do we hold back
from tithing, hesitating to give ourselves wholly?

What kind of king are we expecting when we say Jesus is Lord? Surely
it should not be the same king the Jews of those days expected. It is the
King of a spiritual kingdom where love, not physical power, rules over
everything – a kingdom where the Lord of the cross is at the very centre of
our lives.

It is said that people can love easily, but only until it hurts them. Every
human has this kind of weakness. But the grace of God can work on that
weakness, so long as we admit that weakness to him.

———

To pray:

Lord, you are the Lord of peace and of love. Be the Lord of my life.

Drama of Holy Week

*'The next day the great crowd that had come for the Feast heard that Jesus
was on his way to Jerusalem' (v. 12).*

This year, around 500,000 people will visit Oberammergau in the
Bavarian Alps to view the world famous Passion Play. More than two
thousand local citizens will once again, as they have done regularly since
1634, portray the life of Christ in an open-air theatre. Christ's life, death
and resurrection will come alive for audiences in five-hour productions.

Passion plays succeeded the Easter dramas of the Middle Ages and
focused on the sufferings of Christ. Some included more of the life of
Christ than simply the events of Holy Week. Some playwrights even added
scenes from the Old Testament which foreshadowed the Messiah's coming.
Although often on a smaller scale than Oberammergau's, passion plays are
produced annually in many places around the world. They help us to
visualise the gospel.

Leading up to Good Friday, Palm Sunday would be 'the next day' John
describes in verse 12. The main scene the previous day took place in
Bethany where Jesus and the disciples had supper with Lazarus, Mary and
Martha. A quiet meal with friends became a spectacle. Many came to see
Jesus as well as to see the one he'd raised from death. The chief priests' plot
to kill Jesus widened to include Lazarus because on his account, more Jews
believed in Jesus.

Jesus knew he would die during that year's Passover. Perhaps Mary also
sensed his death was imminent when she anointed his feet with costly
fragrant oil. Her extravagance irritated Judas and others. Jesus said she did
it with his death and burial in mind.

'The next day' Jesus entered Jerusalem as the centre of attention of a
swelling crowd. People hailed him with words taken right from the psalms.
That and everything about the day added to the Pharisees' distress. Their
troubles escalated. They worried among themselves: 'Look how the whole
world has gone after him!' (v. 19).

In the evening, after interacting with crowds in Jerusalem, Jesus and the
disciples returned to Bethany, a retreat less than two miles from the city.
Did the fragrance of devotion linger there and provide comfort for Christ?
Could that be said of our homes?

Spirit of Truth

' "And I will ask the Father, and he will give you another Counsellor to be with you for ever – the Spirit of truth"' (v. 16, 17).

Jesus continues to instruct his disciples. This time he gives them the promise that the Spirit of truth will come to them. This truth will help the disciples to know God and know themselves. One of their problems was that they did not know themselves or Jesus well enough. They did not know that Jesus came not as a king of this world but as the King of hearts and lives. That is why James and John ask Jesus to let them sit at his right and left hand in his glory (see Mark 10:35–37).

When they said 'in your glory' they surely were thinking of worldly glory. Luke's Gospel says: 'A dispute arose among them as to which of them was considered to be greatest' (22:24). These were the disciples who had been following Jesus for three years. Yet they did not know Jesus in a true sense.

They did not know themselves either. They did not know that they were going to forsake Jesus. Peter denied Jesus three times in spite of his declaration in Luke 22:33: 'Lord, I am ready to go with you to prison and to death.' When Jesus was arrested 'everyone deserted him and fled' (Mark 14:50).

But Jesus promised that when the Spirit of truth came they would know Jesus and themselves. His promise was accomplished on the day of Pentecost. The sermon Peter gave on that day (see Acts 2:14–39) shows that Peter is now a changed man who knows the true meaning of Jesus' coming to earth. Later, when Peter and John heal a crippled man at the Gate Beautiful, Peter says, 'Silver or gold I do not have, but what I have I give you. In the name of Jesus Christ of Nazareth, walk' (Acts 3:6).

These words are proof that Peter has received the Spirit of truth. Thank God that he promises the same for us.

———

To pray:

Lord, help us to be open to the Spirit so that we may truly know you and ourselves.

Troubled Hearts

' *"Do not let your hearts be troubled and do not be afraid"*' (v. 27).

Jesus was about to leave his disciples after three years' companionship together. The disciples had followed him, forsaking all they had. Now Jesus is concerned about them and talks to them as though speaking to children. 'Do not let your hearts be troubled. Trust in God; trust also in me. In my Father's house are many rooms; if it were not so, I would have told you' (John 14:1).

Our hearts are troubled when we lose loved ones. I have attended many funerals. For Christians it is a time of victory and return to our heavenly home. Yet it is quite natural to feel sad and for hearts to be troubled.

Jesus knew it and wanted to do something to prepare the hearts of his followers for what would happen when he died. Jesus tells them that he is leaving them but will come back after preparing a place for them. They do not understand everything he says, but Jesus assures them and us that when the Holy Spirit comes he will help us understand everything:

> But the Counsellor, the Holy Spirit, whom the Father will send in my name, will teach you all things and will remind you of everything I have said to you. Peace I leave with you; my peace I give you. I do not give to you as the world gives. Do not let your hearts be troubled and do not be afraid (vv. 26, 27).

What a comfort it is to know that there is a place for each of us and that the Holy Sprit will help us understand all Jesus said!

When his wife died and was about to be taken to the crematorium, a Japanese Christian shouted '*Banzai!*' which can mean 'Hooray!' Some years later when he died, his Christian sister cooked *sekihan*, a special red bean rice which is normally cooked only for celebrations. In Japanese culture it is unheard of to do such things but these faithful Christians knew there was a promised place for their loved ones in Jesus' Father's house.

Prayer topic:

Pray for those who are disturbed by the death of a loved one, that their troubled hearts may be comforted by the Spirit of comfort.

Rise, Let Us Go!

'*"Are you still sleeping and resting? Look, the hour is near, and the Son of Man is betrayed into the hands of sinners. Rise, let us go!"*' (vv. 45, 46).

Gethsemane is the place where Jesus, preparing to take upon himself the sins of the world, faced up to the ultimate trial of his faith, which tested his determination to the ultimate. And during this trial the disciples went to sleep while their Lord most needed their support. They then ran away from his enemies at a time when their Master was sorrowful and troubled.

On another occasion, too, they were less than totally supportive. Matthew tells the story of Jesus sleeping in a boat in a storm. The disciples were afraid and woke him up, saying 'Lord, save us! We're going to drown' (8:25). When they were troubled they woke Jesus up, and yet when Jesus was troubled, they went to sleep.

In the Garden of Gethsemane, Judas came and kissed Jesus. Kissing is a sign of friendliness and affection, but here it became a signal of betrayal. But Jesus the Lord remained in control, declaring: 'Rise, and let us go!' Whatever the plan of Judas may be, however weak the disciples are, still Jesus is Lord of everything. He will be the final victor.

When the Second World War began, The Salvation Army in Japan was ordered to disband, as the military government would allow only a single Christian denomination. The Salvation Army therefore became a part of that denomination. It could not use its name and no Salvationist was allowed to wear Salvation Army uniform. Officers hid them in their houses or buried them in the ground.

Who would have thought that the movement could survive? Sadly some Salvationists gave up their faith, but a couple of years after the end of the war The Salvation Army was re-established and officers who had kept their uniforms came to the re-opening meeting proudly wearing them.

The Lord still instructs us: 'Rise, let us go!' He will always be the final victor and we will share that victory.

Not My Will, But Thine

' "Abba, Father," he said, "everything is possible for you. Take this cup from me. Yet not what I will, but what you will" ' (v. 36).

Gethsemane is the place of agony and victory. Jesus was so troubled that he said, 'My soul is overwhelmed with sorrow to the point of death' (v. 34). Luke says that 'his sweat was like drops of blood falling to the ground' (Luke 22:44).

Jesus' agony was real. As one of The Salvation Army's eleven articles of faith declares, as well as being 'truly and properly God' he was also 'truly and properly man'. When he asked his Father, God: 'Father . . . everything is possible for you. Take this cup from me' (Mark 14:36), his agony was real.

Here is a man who is frightened, troubled, sorrowful. This surely comforts us. Jesus, our Saviour, experienced every trial and sorrow a human might experience. Because of this he can share our fears, sorrows, even our temptations to sin. He himself was tempted to sin, although he did not give in to the temptations (Matthew 4:1–10). 'For we do not have a high priest who is unable to sympathise with our weaknesses, but we have one who has been tempted in every way, just as we are – yet was without sin' (Hebrews 4:15).

Jesus' victory was not only in rising from the dead but also in being able to say: 'Not my will, but thine.'

We must vow with Salvation Army songwriter John Gowans:

> If crosses come, if it should cost me dearly,
> To be the servant of my Servant Lord,
> If darkness falls around the path of duty.
> And men despise the Saviour I've adored.
>
> I'll not turn back, whatever it may cost,
> I'm called to live, to love and save the lost.
> *John Gowans* © The Salvation Army

Carrying the Cross

'Then Jesus said to his disciples, "If anyone would come after me, he must deny himself and take up his cross and follow me"' (v. 24).

One of the requirements of following Jesus is for the disciple to take up his or her cross. Each disciple has an individual cross to carry. Each is different.

Simon of Cyrene was forced to carry the cross of Jesus (Mark 15:21). In doing so, Jesus' cross became his. When we engage in the mission of Christ, we share in his cross.

Let us make Alfred Henry Ackley's words our prayer:

> O let me bear thy cross, dear Lord, I cried,
> And lo, a cross for me appeared;
> The one, forgotten, I had cast aside,
> The one so long that I had feared.
>
> Take up thy cross and follow me,
> I hear the blesséd Saviour call;
> How can I make a lesser sacrifice
> When Jesus gave his all?
>
> (*SASB* [American edition] 978)

Lord, Show Us the Father

' "Lord, show us the Father and that will be enough for us" ' (v. 8).

The Bible offers us little account of the happenings on the Saturday of Holy Week. Two Marys were watching at the tomb after Jesus was buried, probably with dismayed hearts. We imagine that other disciples were feeling the same. We know Jesus was to rise again after three days but they did not. I wonder what they were doing that Saturday.

We experience times when we are lost and do not know what we can do, as we do not know what is coming next. The 'Saturday experience' is the space between the disappointing experience and the restoration from that disappointment.

Two days before the crucifixion, Philip asked Jesus to show them the Father. Jesus responded: 'Don't you know me, Philip, even after I have been among you such a long time?' (v. 9). Philip had to be reminded that he should have seen the Father through Jesus.

The Saturday between Good Friday and Easter Day is a good time to pause to ponder on what Jesus has shown us. Jesus had shown Philip and the other disciples many things in their three years together. We need to reflect on the signs Jesus has shown us in our lives. As we do so we can look forward to the glories of Easter Day.

The 'Saturday experience' gives us time to look at ourselves, too. The disciples may have felt that they were going through a tunnel. At times we feel that way too.

A retired Salvation Army officer pointed out what we see in the window when we are in a train going through a tunnel. We cannot see the countryside, we see only our own face reflected in the glass. At such times we should reflect on our own experience and reaffirm our faith in Christ, remembering what he did for us.

———————

To pray:

Let us not be afraid of seeing our true selves, but rely on you, Lord, and reaffirm what you have done for us.

Hearts Burning

' "*Were not our hearts burning while he talked with us on the road and opened the Scriptures to us?*" ' (v. 32).

After the death of Jesus the hearts of the disciples were weak and dismayed. They were disappointed with what had happened to Jesus; it was quite different from what they expected. Here we see two disciples who are leaving Jerusalem and going down to a village called Emmaus with a sense of disappointment and despair.

At that very moment Jesus walked with them. The glorious implication for us is that the risen Lord who became their companion will be our companion on our road too.

> He lives, he lives,
> Christ Jesus lives today!
> He walks with me and talks with me
> Along life's narrow way.
> He lives, he lives,
> Salvation to impart!
> You ask me how I know he lives?
> He lives within my heart!
> *Alfred Henry Ackley* (*SASB* 334)

When we see the risen Lord revealed in Scripture and he talks with us, our hearts always burn. If we do not see him there immediately, let's read the Scripture until he reveals himself to us. On this Easter Sunday let us sense the reality of the risen Lord again through his Word.

―――――――――

To pray:

Lord, help us to see you as clearly as the two for whom you explained the Scripture on that first Easter. May our hearts too burn with the truth!

A Box of Paradox – Surprises of the Kingdom

Introduction

Due in part to the culture and customs of the Middle East at the time when Scripture was written, its method of teaching is sometimes unfamiliar to today's reader, especially those in Western cultures. Answering questions with questions or presenting paradoxical statements was common practice.

From our viewpoint, paradox may sometimes seem inimical to truth. But Jesus used many such opposites to teach the surprising nature of the kingdom of God. Elton Trueblood said: 'If a man wishes to avoid the disturbing effect of paradoxes, the best advice is for him to leave the Christian faith alone.' If we are willing to live with the tension of truth expressed in paradox, we'll be richer.

At first, paradoxes seem to be contradictory, but are entirely true. When Dr Richard A. Swenson[15] says, 'Our sense of the presence of God is inversely proportional to the speed of our lives' we know it is true even though it seems counterintuitive. There are paradoxes in nature: the sun that softens the wax hardens the clay. It's not surprising that Jesus employed inversions to teach eternal truth about giving and living. Paul did so as well (Philippians 3:7).

It was also common practice in the Old Testament. Psalm 113 tells of God's gracious dealings with the downtrodden, whom he seats in juxtaposition with princes (vv. 7, 8). He proclaims the anomaly of the barren woman whom God makes the happy mother of children.

Parallel truths, like parallel lines, meet only at infinity, beyond our sight. Since earthly experience is partial and subjective, perhaps the Lord gives us an inkling of his frame of reference to prepare us for heaven. 'He puts a little of heaven in our hearts so that we'll never settle for less' (2 Corinthians 5:5, *MSG*).

Prized Wheat

'Let both grow together until the harvest. At that time I will tell the harvesters: First collect the weeds and tie them in bundles to be burned; then gather the wheat and bring it into my barn' (v. 30).

Radio interviews with mathematics professors about new theories amaze us. Our minds are stretched or baffled by the discussions in a different dimension. A mathematician best known by his pseudonym, Lewis Carroll, toyed with logic and presented it in a whimsical way in his children's book, *Alice in Wonderland*, in which the unexpected happened regularly and facts were portrayed in amusing juxtaposition.

Occasionally we have noted paradoxes of the kingdom in the *Words of Life* comments. The Gospels are full of juxtapositions and seeming paradoxes. When people first heard some of the things Jesus said, they must have wondered if they could be true: blessed are they that mourn; unless you become as children you cannot enter the kingdom of heaven; the first shall be last and the last first.

Regarding such paradoxes, writer Philip Yancey says: 'All these profound principles of life appear in the New Testament and none easily reduces to logical consistency.'[16]

Jesus taught in parables. Perhaps that approach helps ease the strain of radical spiritual concepts. He teaches that we live in a complex world. Wheat and weeds coexist, even thrive. Although it's unfair, sometimes the weeds surpass the wheat. We know this is true physically and concede the metaphors for spiritual life.

Jesus reminds us that it is he who sows the good seed. He knows what he's planted will in the end destroy the weeds and he will harvest his prized crop, us. God sets great store by his faithful followers. The truth stuns us and surpasses our reckoning.

Retired Salvation Army General John Gowans comments:

One of the paradoxes of our faith is that God stands ready to provide all the help we need to live successful, fulfilled and meaningful lives – and wants nothing more than to do so – but he will not force his aid upon us. Five millennia of history reveal that if men and women choose to go their own way, he will not intervene. He loves us too much to take back his gift of free will.

Heart Scan

'But the LORD said to Samuel, "Do not consider his appearance or his height,
for I have rejected him. The LORD does not look at the things man looks at.
Man looks at the outward appearance, but the LORD looks at the heart"' (v. 7).

Seeming inversions appear frequently in Scripture. It isn't surprising since our human, limited viewpoints and automatic assumptions are so different from divine views.

God sees differently and wants us to see things his way. A Japanese proverb says, 'Though in rags, he has a heart of brocade.' It reminds us of the familiar words of our key verse which God spoke to Samuel at the selection of David as second king of Israel. The fact is simultaneously reassuring and challenging.

It is challenging when we remember that God sees our hearts and minds more thoroughly than the best airport screening detects the keys in our pocket. It is reassuring when we consider that no matter what others think of us, God knows our hearts and motives.

Shortly before Holy Week, when he and his disciples were near the temple in Jerusalem, Jesus sat and watched people giving their offerings. He saw the wealthy giving substantially, but also noticed a poor woman giving little. The disciples probably didn't notice her or her gift.

It must have surprised them when Jesus called them to him and commended her giving. What he said showed that he knew her heart. It was a matter of proportion. The rich had given out of their wealth but still had plenty left for themselves. She had given out of her poverty and had nothing left but her devotion to God. Jesus said that she'd actually given more than the rich had.

Society tells us that more is the goal. Car bumper stickers quip: 'He who dies with the most toys wins.' Advertisements entice us to want more of everything as if having the latest gadget or garb will gain us elusive happiness at last. Jesus counters that life is not made up of heaps of things (Luke 12:15).

———

To ponder:

If I love and trust the One who knows me inside out, how does my lifestyle reflect that faith today?

Incredible

'Now to him who is able to do immeasurably more than all we ask or imagine, according to his power that is at work within us, to him be glory in the church and in Christ Jesus throughout all generations, for ever and ever! Amen' (vv. 20, 21).

When Jesus fed more than four thousand people with seven loaves and some fish there were seven baskets of leftovers. He fed more than five thousand with five loaves and two fish and there were twelve baskets of leftovers. With fewer resources and greater need, God's provision was greater. There were even more leftovers. It seems counterintuitive. We puzzle over how this can be.

Zacchaeus's conversion story is well known. On 4 February we considered the new maths of that changed man whose new life and new-found generosity immediately started to reflect God's way of calculating.

We have a limited view of God's resources, but Paul reminds the Philippians and us: 'My God will meet all your needs according to his glorious riches in Christ Jesus' (4:19). How can this be? Isn't it because our needs are met on God's terms, according to his riches in Christ, therefore from a limitless supply?

It is also true that those who revere God and take refuge in him are kept in his 'secret place' that the psalmists write about (Psalm 27:5; 31:19, 20; 91). If we are in Christ and our resources are in Christ, we, our needs and our means of supply are together in the same place.

This is mind-boggling. God says it best: 'As the heavens are higher than the earth, so are my ways higher than your ways and my thoughts than your thoughts' (Isaiah 55:9). Even what little we understand leaves us in awe and overwhelmed. Yet, knowing that God loves us and has the best in mind for us, we don't despair, but delight in a God who is greater than we can imagine. As Salvationist songwriter Howard Davies reminds us:

> Higher than the stars that reach eternity,
> Broader than the boundaries of endless space,
> Is the boundless love of God that pardoned me;
> O the wonder of his grace!
>
> (*SASB* 52)

Strength in Weakness

'But those who wait upon GOD get fresh strength' (Isaiah 40:31, MSG).

It's obvious that God works differently than we do and wants us to cooperate with his way. Our usual approach for gaining knowledge and decreasing ignorance is to study hard, even relentlessly; for increasing athletic skills, practise more, even fiercely.

Although spiritual disciplines can be helpful tools, they are not as important in God's plan for our spiritual life as living a life of trusting him. No amount of trying harder will bring us to heaven or to peace with him. His way for us is to listen to him, obey him and trust him – in short to depend upon him more than on ourselves or our endeavours.

It may seem illogical, but we learn that the basis of grace is not more effort. In answer to Paul's prayer for healing, the Lord replies: 'My grace is sufficient for you, for my power is made perfect in weakness' (v. 9). There's a paradox! Paul was judicious enough to embrace God's way. He was even able to say:

> Therefore I will boast all the more gladly about my weaknesses, so that Christ's power may rest on me. That is why, for Christ's sake, I delight in weaknesses, in insults, in hardships, in persecutions, in difficulties. For when I am weak, then I am strong (vv. 9, 10).

In an earlier age when national security involved well-trained, fully equipped mobilised armies, David learned the wisdom of relying on the unseen God rather than amassed forces. He boldly declares: 'Some trust in chariots and some in horses, but we trust in the name of the LORD our God' (Psalm 20:7).

In Zechariah 4:6 the heavenly messenger gives Zerubbabel God's message: 'This is the word of the LORD to Zerubbabel: "Not by might nor by power, but by my Spirit," says the LORD Almighty.' As we cooperate with God's methods, to our wonder, by his Spirit, he accomplishes things for our good and of eternal value.

To pray:

Lord, help me to believe that my fragility, placed in your keeping, gives others opportunity to glimpse your strength. I trust you for this today.

Losers Keepers

'But whoever loses his life for me will find it' (v. 25).

The American television reality series, *Biggest Loser*, gathers overweight people from across the country. The team that sheds the most pounds wins a substantial cash prize. For this programme, only one team is champion, but effectively all the losers are winners.

Jesus offers his followers a paradoxical 'lose to win' opportunity. As *The Message* states it:

> Anyone who intends to come with me has to let me lead. You're not in the driver's seat; *I* am. Don't run from suffering; embrace it. Follow me and I'll show you how. Self-help is no help at all. Self-sacrifice is the way, my way, to finding yourself, your true self (Matthew 16:24, 25).

Some have fleshed out taking up their cross daily and following Christ in notable ways. Others have done it less dramatically or publicly, yet just as poignantly. For some it entails doing menial tasks in Jesus' name.

A poor and uneducated clumsy former soldier and footman, Nicholas Herman of Lorraine, France, thought if he joined a monastery he could be disciplined for some of his awkwardness and faults. He became a lay Carmelite brother in Paris in 1666, taking the name Brother Lawrence. He had an aversion to the kitchen work to which he was assigned at the monastery for fifteen years. Yet by doing his assignment for the love of God, with prayer and depending on God's grace, he found the tasks were bearable and became a means of communion with God. 'I began to live as if there were no one save God and me in the world,' he said.

He gained through losing. He believed if he could, then anyone could live this way anywhere. No special training or church ritual is required. Some of the wisdom Brother Lawrence passed on to those who sought his guidance was posthumously compiled in *The Practice of the Presence of God*. The classic, recommended by John Wesley and others, is still available.

To pray:

Lord, help me to practise your presence here today.

105

Holy Lowly King

'Take my yoke upon you and learn of me, for I am gentle (meek) and humble (lowly) in heart, and you will find rest (relief and ease and refreshment and recreation and blessed quiet) for your souls' (v. 29, AB).

A child mistakenly sings 'lowly, lowly, lowly' instead of 'holy, holy, holy'. Yet the truth she sings reminds us of another paradox of the kingdom. A number of carols include the word 'lowly' when describing the Saviour's humble birth. We hear 'lowly' echoed in hymns connected with Palm Sunday. Henry Hart Milman writes, 'Ride on, ride on in majesty! In lowly pomp ride on to die' and we sense the paradox of our exalted and humble King Jesus.

Jesus personifies lowliness and humility. He also holds it up as a valuable trait for his followers to possess. Consider another incident during Holy Week when he washed his disciples' feet and explained that although he was their teacher, he had done a humble service for them. They should meet others' needs in like manner.

It is both reassuring and perplexing to encounter a Christ who chooses to take a lowly place among us with 'nowhere to lay his head' (Matthew 8:20).

Japanese Christian activist Toyohiko Kagawa lived for nineteen years in a six foot by six foot shack in the slums. The government made him Chief of Social Welfare to organise the formidable task of rebuilding Tokyo after the 1923 earthquake which left millions homeless. Kagawa turned down the sizable wage because he felt that, following Christ's example, to work with the poor he must be poor as well.

In one of his pastoral letters to Salvationists worldwide, about humility, General Shaw Clifton wrote:

The English word humility comes from the Latin *humus* meaning earth or soil. It refers to something lowly, something beneath our feet. It thus becomes an antidote to pride. Before Jesus was born, the Romans and Greeks were scornful of humility. It was something found only in slaves and in others of low station in life. Yet Jesus embraced it. Because he did so, humility was transformed from a mark of social degradation to an essential Christian virtue.

More than Wonderful

*'How precious to me are your thoughts, O God! How vast is the sum of them!
Were I to count them, they would outnumber the grains of sand. When I
awake, I am still with you' (vv. 17, 18).*

In Psalm 139 David writes four distinct stanzas with four themes. He
recounts the omniscience, omnipresence and omnipotence of God
related to his life and then shows how these stir his fidelity.

From the outset the psalmist recognises that God has examined him
thoroughly and knows everything about him: 'I'm an open book to you'
(v. 1, *MSG*). God knows his actions, his speech, his thoughts, his motives,
and has done, right from conception. To be known so intimately by God
doesn't disconcert him, but amazes, challenges and heartens him.

Confident in God's nature and purpose, David courageously invites
God to examine him inside out again: 'Investigate my life, O God, find out
everything about me; Cross-examine and test me, get a clear picture of
what I'm about' and concludes: 'then guide me on the road to eternal life'
(v. 23, 24, *MSG*). Dare we ask the same?

An Inward Realm

There is an inward realm beyond my dreams,
Below the surface of my conscious thought,
Where God can dwell, composing mighty themes
Surpassing far those themes which I have wrought.
If I but cease to struggle and to strain
And let him move the bars from round my cell,
And burst the fetters which my soul enchain
And let his touch my apprehensions quell.

Then will I know the joy transcending speech,
The holiness which only Christ can give,
The faith which always seemed far past my reach,
Love's mystery, Christ's gift to make me live.

Lord, play thy mighty music in my soul,
And set me free, to live in thy control.

Harry Read

Truth in Extremes

*'The LORD is close to the broken-hearted and saves those who
are crushed in spirit' (Psalm 34:18).*

Jesus' Sermon on the Mount is a collection of surprising declarations,
paradoxes – none more so than the Beatitudes. Salvationist poet Arch R.
Wiggins paraphrases the Beatitudes in song. The first of three verses recaps:

> Blessed are the poor in spirit,
> They the Kingdom shall possess;
> Blessed are the broken-hearted,
> They shall not be comfortless;
> Blessed are the meek and lowly,
> Theirs the earth by right shall be;
> Blessed they who thirst for goodness,
> They shall drink abundantly.
>
> (*SASB* 95)

What Jesus said wasn't a departure from what God had said through Old
Testament writers. Hundreds of years earlier, their forefathers heard
Isaiah's message:

For this is what the high and lofty One says – he who lives for ever,
whose name is holy: 'I live in a high and holy place, but also with him
who is contrite and lowly in spirit, to revive the spirit of the lowly and
to revive the heart of the contrite' (Isaiah 57:15).

Even though we are learning to live with paradox, doesn't this amaze us as
well? G. K. Chesterton said: 'Christianity got over the difficulty of combining furious opposites by keeping them both and keeping them both furious.'

As Christians, our Lord's death is our means to new life. The indispen-
sable bad news generates the incredible good news. They can only both be
true because Christ is fully God and fully human, because God is
sovereign, yet gives us free will. We hold the mystery of such tensions, truth
in extremes reverently.

One of the delightful surprises of the kingdom is that the Lord of all is
still close to the broken-hearted. He still comes to the childlike, humble and
penitent.

In the Midst

*'God is in the midst of her, she shall not be moved; God shall help her,
just at the break of dawn' (Psalm 46:5, NKJV)*

'In the midst' can express a location. That could be the simple meaning of the psalmist's words: 'In the midst of the congregation will I praise you' (Psalm 22:22, *AB*). 'In the midst' can also relate to a situation. When I say I'm in the midst of something I usually mean I'm busy with a task which still needs my attention. I'm in the midst of writing this edition, this daily thought.

Formerly the phrase also described a point during an interval of time. 'In the midst of his years' meant the prime of a person's life. Jesus came to the disciples on the lake one night in the midst of the sea (place) and the midst of the storm (state and time).

Jesus offers peace in the midst of our present-day storms. Writer Philip Yancey reminds us:

Living as resident aliens in a strange land, citizens of a secret kingdom, what other kind of peace should we expect? When Jesus' mother encountered things she could not rationally resolve, she held them inside her soul, 'pondering' them, carrying the tension rather than trying to eliminate it.[16]

How is it that God, who is the completely 'Other', whose mind is unknowable (Romans 11:33–36), whom no one can instruct, who lives in a high and holy place, condescends to work 'salvation in the midst of the earth' (Psalm 74:12, *AB*)? Jeanne Guyon said: 'If knowing answers to life's questions is absolutely necessary to you, then forget the journey. This is a journey of unknowables – of unanswered questions, enigmas, incomprehensibles, and most of all, things unfair.'[17]

For now we live in paradoxes that puzzle and confound us, but need not overwhelm us. We know Christ. He comes to us 'in the midst' with comfort and truth. We say yes to him. He leads us. There is still mystery, but it leads us humbly to worship him (See John 20:19, 20).

Happiest Giver

*'You'll not likely go wrong here if you keep remembering that our Master said,
"You're far happier giving than getting"'* (v. 35, MSG).

Paul summons the leaders of the church at Ephesus for a moving
farewell address. He says he hasn't coveted others' things. He has
supported himself and his companions with his own labour. He advises
them to seek opportunities to help the weak and uses the familiar paradox
of our key verse: 'It is more blessed to give than to receive.' Paul attributes
the words to Christ, although they are not recorded in the Gospels.

This paradox is hard for children. 'Why do we have to offer the biggest
piece of cake to our friends when they visit us and then be happy to take
the smallest piece when we're at their house?' It's not easy for adults either.
Can we actually want to be generous when we don't have to be? Yes. As
Major Howard Webber wrote in the UK Territory's *Salvationist*: 'When we
are filled with the Spirit of God, giving and the joyful desire to do so
become part of our nature.'

People may surprise us in the way they show gratitude: 'Please sir, I
want some more.' Perhaps if we asked the Lord for more of his spiritual
nourishment it would please him as well. Awareness of another's needs
may mean considering the recipient's feelings and whether what we offer
causes a burden of obligation heavier than the gift warrants. Anonymous
giving, or at least giving without expecting anything in return, reflects
God's nature.

John records God's priceless invitation to wholeness and restoration:
'Let those who are thirsty come; and let all who wish take the free gift of
the water of life' (Revelation 22:17, *TNIV*). Earlier John had recorded
Jesus' similar call to the crowds in Jerusalem (John 7:37). Both echoed
what God said through Isaiah hundreds of years earlier: 'Come, all you
who are thirsty, come to the waters; and you who have no money, come,
buy and eat!' (Isaiah 55:1).

Our times protest: nothing can be free. No one is that generous. But
we're talking about God whose ways are matchless. By his own criteria, he
must be the happiest giver in the universe. We follow him.

Grace of Giving

'The world of the generous gets larger and larger; the world of the stingy gets smaller and smaller' (Proverbs 11:24, MSG).

We considered Jesus seeing the motives of the givers at the temple (6 April). Earlier in his ministry in Galilee he warned against giving as the hypocrites do, seeking human approval and praise. He counsels not to let our left hand know what our right does. That paradox suggests giving secretly, for God alone.

Jesus says that God sees and will reward such giving. Luke's account of what Jesus said in Galilee includes another aspect of the paradox: 'Give, and it will be given to you. A good measure, pressed down, shaken together and running over, will be poured into your lap. For with the measure you use, it will be measured to you' (Luke 6:38). This is not a 'give to get' scheme, but one with undeserved benefits.

Part of the joy of giving is being surprised at God's unexpected rewards. When can we anticipate reward – now, later or possibly both? Individuals with savings can choose among several schemes for gaining interest. Usually there's an advantage for those willing to wait for access to their money.

Dr John N. Oswalt, research professor of Old Testament at Wesley Biblical Seminary, writes about spiritual rewards promised in Isaiah 62:

> Still, we should not think that his 'reward' is only at the end of time or after death. Those who live their lives as expressions of Spirit-empowered righteousness have their reward in themselves day after day, as they live in unbroken communion with their God, for they are his 'holy people' (v.12), the realisation of his creation plan, and the fulfilment of his covenant goal.[18]

What, when and how we should give are matters of the heart and need divine direction. Once Jesus told his host to invite people to dine who had no way to repay him and promised there would be reward later (Luke 14:14). In another place he says people who aid Christians simply with a cup of water will be rewarded. Someone has said that a miser just hoards the wrong things in the wrong place. Jesus calls us to stockpile treasure in heaven (Matthew 6:19–21). His rewards are now and later.

Deep Cleansing Agent

' "*Come now, let us reason together,*" *says the* LORD. "*Though your sins are like scarlet, they shall be as white as snow; though they are red as crimson, they shall be like wool*" ' *(Isaiah 1:18).*

Just two weeks ago Christians around the world contemplated the events of Good Friday. Christ's death and resurrection are foundational to Christian theology and especially Paul's New Testament teaching. The cross is the ultimate and pivotal paradox – the God Man, Jesus Christ, intentionally gives his sinless life to pay for the sins of humanity. He now demonstrates the love for his enemies that he taught. He dies that we may live.

The way of the cross tells us that just as surely as God is sovereign, humankind is responsible to choose or reject God's offer of salvation. Paradoxically, his sovereignty and our responsibility co-exist. God may do as he pleases and our part is to do what pleases God. Even the possibility of being cleansed from sin is God's merciful gift.

Some stains will come out only with the use of special products or processes; others won't come out at all. Even water, the universal solvent, doesn't always work. Our key verse talks about tough stains. God tells us that the double-dyed red stains of both our tendency to sin and our specific sins can be expunged and the fabric of our lives made as clean as a snowy white, freshly shorn, well-cleansed fleece.

Mark describes Jesus' glistening garments at the time of his transfiguration as more sparkling than any cleaner on earth could launder or bleach them. In Revelation, John tells of the believers in heaven whose robes are washed white in the blood of the Lamb.

Hebrews 9 refers back to the Exodus account and reminds us: 'In fact, the law requires that nearly everything be cleansed with blood, and without the shedding of blood there is no forgiveness' (v. 22).

We marvel at the metaphor – blood which usually stains, cleanses. Only God can accomplish this divine paradox. So, grateful for the cleansing blood of Christ, we pray confidently with the penitent David: 'Cleanse me with hyssop, and I will be clean; wash me, and I will be whiter than snow' (Psalm 51:7).

Indeed

*'Jesus looked at them and said, "With man this is impossible,
but with God all things are possible"' (v. 26).*

Jesus states that God can handle what people consider impossible situations. Then he reassures his disciples that in the final analysis, the rewards for those who sacrificially follow him will be manifold – totally out of proportion to what they forfeit. Also, they shouldn't be surprised to find things out of their customary sequence.

In her poem 'Odd Couples',[19] poet Luci Shaw calls a few paradoxes of Christian faith mixed metaphors:

> things are so often
> at odds with their containers:
>
> > our cat once nested her young
> > in a bureau drawer,
> >
> > the copper kettle on the shelf
> > is boiling with partridge berries,
> >
> > my eye sips baby tears that leak
> > over a china rim.
>
> other mixed metaphors rush
> to be recognized:
>
> > that baby in the corn crib,
> > God in a sweaty body,
> >
> > eternity spilled the third day
> > from a hole in the hill,
> >
> > for you – a painter-plumber,
> > me – a poet sorting socks,
> >
> > all of us, teetotallers drunk
> > on the Holy Ghost.

113

Emboldened to Trust

'The LORD will fulfil his purpose for me; your love, O LORD, endures for ever' (v. 8).

David aptly begins the psalm with praise to God. If we wonder what causes him to burst into praise, we find his reason in verse 3. At a certain time when he prayed for help, God answered him and strengthened him for that occasion. This in turn encouraged his faith. David believes that others who hear what God did for him will give God credit as well.

He continues that although it is hard to imagine, such a wonderful, mighty God takes time to care for the humblest person. David is confident that whatever trouble comes his way, God is available to help and strengthen him. In the broader picture, David is confident that the Lord's loving greater plan for his life will be accomplished.

Where does our life intersect with this psalm? Individuals or groups keeping prayer journals can quickly point to evidence of the Lord's specific answers to specific prayers. That practice encourages the pray-ers. The victories engender more prayer. Remembering what God has done for us in the past inspires our confidence in his intentions of good for our future.

Perhaps today is a good time to take this brief psalm verse by verse and personalise its words in answer to a few questions:

* What stirs me to praise God?
* When did I recently call on God and receive an answer that strengthened me for my challenges?
* How have I recently acknowledged God's work in my life in a way that encouraged someone else to trust him too?
* Does verse 6 comfort or trouble me?
* Based on past experience and God's matchless ability, can I sincerely tell him, as the psalmist does in verses 7 and 8, that I trust him for the days ahead?

As for the psalmist's closing plea that God would not desert his handiwork, Paul assures Christians: 'For we are God's masterpiece. He has created us anew in Christ Jesus, so we can do the good things he planned for us long ago' (Ephesians 2:10, *NLT*).

More from Mark

(chapters 5–8)

Introduction

A s we pick up Mark's account again, Jesus and the disciples are disembarking on the east side of the Sea of Galilee in unfamiliar territory. After the disquieting storm at sea and witnessing Jesus' astonishing ability to calm the waves, they are safe on land once more. They might expect that any queasiness would be set right now that they are on firm ground, but surprising events continue.

We follow Jesus and the disciples as they spend much of their time outside Galilee. Jesus directs his attention to instructing his followers and revealing more about who he really is. The crucial passage in Mark 8 is the culminating point to which the first half of Mark's Gospel rises and from which the second half flows.

Beyond Galilee

'So the man went away and began to tell in the Decapolis how much Jesus had done for him. And all the people were amazed' (v. 20).

The region was called Decapolis because of its ten cities, established by Greeks, conquered by Jews and liberated by Romans. We imagine that the customs and language of the people reflected some of the area's history. The mixed population meant that in that area some farmers kept pigs.

After a memorable night at sea the party comes ashore, possibly before daylight, near the 'home' of a naked man who lives among hillside caves used as a cemetery. Mark gives vivid detail of the incident that ensues, no doubt based on Peter's eyewitness report. He devotes more space to the account than either Matthew or Luke.

Again Mark tells us that something happens *immediately*. When Jesus gets out of the boat, in an eerie reception, the man who screams and cuts himself night and day runs to meet him. The man howls and calls Jesus 'Son of the Most High God' – a term Gentiles used to refer to Israel's God in Old Testament times. He bellows because Jesus has already diagnosed his trouble and told the demon to come out of him.

Jesus does not shout back at the troubled man, but asks his name. The man replies, 'Legion.' Aside from the degree of torment he experiences, has he seen Roman legions, regiments of thousands of soldiers, in action? Has he been a victim of some military abuse of power?

Jesus allows the demons their request – to enter a herd of pigs which promptly rush down the bank and drown in the lake. This dramatically demonstrates to the man that they are gone and he is free. The news travels. People come to the site, see the now sane man and are afraid. They want the change agent to leave.

The restored man wants to follow his healer. Instead Jesus sends him into the region to testify. Since he is a Gentile and his proclamation is in a Gentile area where Jesus would not continue to minister, Jesus doesn't restrain the freed man from spreading the good news. What a formidable yet fearless witness the man would make!

Garments of Praise

'To give them the garment of praise for the spirit of heaviness'
(Isaiah 61:3, NKJV).

When the town's people came out near the lake to see the previously deranged man, he was completely changed. Instead of running, he was sitting. Instead of ranting, he was in his right mind. Instead of looking wild, he was clothed (v. 15). We aren't told the source of his attire. Perhaps the disciples shared theirs.

As Jesus and his followers took a return daylight trip across the lake to Galilee, the disciples could discuss the miraculous encounter with the man as well as their earlier experience in the storm. No doubt they wanted more time with Christ. But as usual, as soon as he was spotted, a large crowd gathered around him at the shore. The crowd stayed with him as he accompanied a desperate father home to the deathbed of his young daughter. But a desperate woman in the crowd captured the Master's attention first.

Her chronic health problem had also become a financial, social and religious burden. The Jewish law declared her ceremonially unclean. Perhaps her feet hurt from standing since anything she sat on became classified as unclean. Perhaps her clothes were all but worn out from constant washing. Any new clothes she had were folded away with her dreams. She kept her distance so that others wouldn't touch her and become defiled.

But she thinks that if she just touches Christ, she'll be healed. So as a last resort she works her way from the fringe of the crowd through to Jesus. She reaches for the back of his robe. She doesn't contaminate him. Rather, Mark says that *immediately* she senses healing. Her dream is realised.

Although he does not see her, Jesus knows *at once* and turns around to find out to whom his healing power has gone. Only the woman knows that he knows. In awe of him and in gratitude for her healing, she publicly admits her deed (v. 33).

Jesus uniquely addresses her with the endearing term of 'daughter'. In confirmation of her experience she hears the kindest words she's heard in years and the prized words of hope and promise: 'Your faith has made you well. Your suffering is over' (v. 34, *NLT*). Hallelujah! It's time to take out folded-away dreams.

Only a Carpenter?

*'He could not do any miracles there . . . and . . . he was amazed
at their lack of faith' (vv. 5, 6).*

After Jesus restores the life of the daughter of Jairus in Capernaum, he heads for Nazareth. Nowadays people move frequently – not just those in the military or ministry. Fewer live in or near their place of birth or childhood. Many might find it hard to claim a hometown. Not so with Jesus.

His family was from Nazareth. Although born in Bethlehem, he spent most of his life in Nazareth. He would have played, worked, socialised, worshipped in its vicinity. We don't know why people spoke of this Galilean town disparagingly. Even others from Galilee, such as disciple Nathanael, initially questioned if anything good could come from Nazareth (John 1:45, 46).

On this visit home Jesus is accompanied by disciples – a rabbi surrounded by his pupils. On the Sabbath they go to the synagogue where he had sometime before startled the assembled when he read a Messianic passage from Isaiah and said it was fulfilled in him. The reaction that time was rage. People drove him out of town (Luke 4). Now he is on a public mission and preparing his followers for theirs. What reception does he receive?

People are suspicious of his teaching. When they say he's only a carpenter and Mary's son, they belittle his roots as a common labourer, and one born under abnormal circumstances. They're suspicious of his learning and his ability to do miracles. Such power had to come from God or Satan. They can't believe he's of God.

Faith is still a requisite of the kingdom of God.

> If in a simple carpenter
> You see the Son of God
> If you would choose to lose
> When you could win;
> If you would give your life away
> For nothing in return
> Then you are where
> My kingdom will begin.[20]

Preparation and After Care

' *"Come with me by yourselves to a quiet place and get some rest"* ' *(v. 31)*.

After his hometown rejection, Jesus probably never returns to Nazareth. The unbelief of family and friends disappoints him, yet he proceeds with his mission, teaching from town to town. This tour also gives him opportunity for more mentoring, more preparation of the disciples who would extend his ministry.

One day Jesus gathers the disciples around him. They may sit randomly within earshot while he explains their task, but he then pairs them off and sends them out in teams. Two can provide moral and physical support to each other. Also, the testimony of two witnesses can stand up legally. The disciples become his official representatives. He gives them spiritual authority for a special mission and expects them to bring back a report, to be accountable for their time and effort.

For this particular mission he instructs that they take the minimum, essential, functional kit. Travel light. Trust God. Take offered hospitality. Testify against those who reject the message. So with full awareness that they wouldn't succeed with everyone, they set off. They follow Christ's example of simplicity in their focused mission. They preach repentance and demonstrate the power of God when they drive out demons and heal the sick.

When they report back to Christ they relate all they did and taught. Imagine them interrupting each other to fill in the details. No doubt they learned a great deal about ministry in a hands-on mission on their own. By honest evaluation in Christ's presence they have opportunity to more fully comprehend what has happened.

Jesus recognises needs the disciples have overlooked. They are wound up and overtired. The usual demands of the crowds that surround Jesus mean they don't even have a chance to eat. He invites them to come away and rest. How relieved they must be to board a boat and push off for a peaceful ride to an out-of-the-way place with Jesus. The rhythm of the waves calms their chatter.

Even a brief time without distractions which are rife in our lives is palliative. The rhythms of creation restore us, but we need distraction-free time with our Creator, too, especially after times of intense ministry. May God help us to plan intervals of quietness.

119

By His Hands, All Are Fed

' "How many loaves of bread do you have? Take an inventory." That didn't
take long. "Five," they said, "plus two fish" ' (v. 38, MSG).

The disciples' quiet respite turns out to be only for as long as the ride on
the lake lasts. People who recognise them anticipate their destination,
sprint along the shore and beat them to their 'solitary place' on the
northeast shore. We don't know what the disciples initially think about the
crowd, but Jesus' reaction is compassionate and suited to what he knows
they need. Spiritually they are like sheep that are disorientated,
directionless and defenceless. So he offers clear teaching.

The sun starts to dip behind the western hills when the disciples remark
on the lateness of the hour and the remoteness of the area. They ask Jesus
to disperse the crowd so the several thousand can find food. On the
contrary, he suggests they feed the people. Their minds race to calculate
the cost. It will be so expensive.

Instead of focusing on the cost, Jesus asks them to see what there is at
hand (v. 38). He plans to teach them a lesson about starting with incredibly
small resources and relying on God. They find barely enough food for a
poor boy's snack: barley bread and two small salt-fish. Surely Jesus will
send the people away now. Instead, he tells his followers to have them sit in
groups.

The Greek word for 'groups' or sections here is similar to a word for
orderly vegetable garden plots. Imagine people seated on the green grass
in straight rows. Mark's mention of the area's green grass helps set the
event in late spring, mid-April.

Jesus as host offers the blessing; that is, he praises God. Jesus looks to
heaven while the food is still snack-size and shows total dependence on
God to provide enough for everyone. He breaks the bread and divides the
fish, and then it starts to happen. The food multiplies in Jesus' hands.
There's ample for the disciples to distribute to the groups.

When everyone is full, the twelve find plenty left over to fill their own
wicker hand baskets. *Immediately* Jesus hurries them to the boat and sends
them off. Perhaps they eat on board and reflect on the incredible 'retreat'
day never to be forgotten. This is the only miracle recorded in all four
Gospels.

It's All Right, I'm Here. Hush Now

' "It's all right, it is I myself; don't be afraid!" ' (v. 50, JBP).

Jesus may send the disciples ahead and dismiss the crowds himself because of a popular move he knows is stirring to make him king (John 6:15). If the disciples get caught up in such a nationalistic outburst, they could complicate things. But outside of exercising effective crowd release, Jesus wants time alone. While the nourished crowds make their way home and the disciples row toward the next appointed location, Jesus prays.

More than being drained by demands of his intense healing and teaching ministry, Jesus is under scrutiny and pressure. Jewish leadership is hostile toward him, Herod is suspicious of him and zealots want to make him their liberator. He needs to renew his perspective and replenish his strength.

Those closest to him note that Jesus praises God publicly; teaches about the importance of persistent, specific, expectant, private prayer; furnishes a sample, timeless prayer; spontaneously bursts into conversation with the Father at critical moments; promises to ask the Father to send the Spirit for his followers' comfort; in the garden agonises over the cross; from the cross cries out for forgiveness for his enemies and entrusts his spirit to his Father.

But do they know how often he slips away from others to be alone for prayer? When everyone has gone, Jesus intentionally goes in another direction, up a mountain to pray in solitude. We don't know how long he prayed, but when he sees his friends still on the lake in the night struggling to row against the wind, he goes to them. It isn't a storm at sea with Jesus asleep in the stern. This time the disciples contend with a contrary wind without Jesus.

They need him, so why don't they recognise him when he comes to them? He comes in an unexpected way, walking on the water. Their first reaction is a shriek of fear at seeing what they think is a ghost. Mark tells us that *immediately* Jesus encourages them and identifies himself. In Greek it only takes three words. When he gets in the boat and the wind dies down, any doubts as to who he is are quelled. They're completely dumbfounded.

Life's winds buffet us. We struggle. Jesus knows, cares and is near. He speaks his calming triplet to us too: Take courage, I AM, fear not. Will we trust him?

121

Perfectly Restored in Thee

'In hope that the creation itself will be liberated from its bondage to decay and brought into the glorious freedom of the children of God' (Romans 8:20, 21).

The recently observed Earth Day drew awareness to our fragile planet. There seems to be both reason for hope and concern when thinking about our global home. Some polluted sites have been cleaned up, but will their ecosystems ever be fully restored? Through conservation programmes, some previously 'endangered' species are now only 'threatened', but what about those already extinct?

In certain countries, today is Creation Sunday. It's appropriate to think about our role in the stewardship of God's gift of creation. Even in its fallen state, the cosmos, in its beauty and bounty, is the work of our personal and loving Creator. Picking up rubbish, conserving power, saving vegetable peelings for compost for the garden may not seem much, but they're simple acts that cooperate with the Creator in his garden, our earthly home.

In today's psalm the exiles mourn the loss of their homeland. They find singing impossible while Jerusalem is in ruins and they are unable to restore her. They hang their harps on the willow trees, which are also a symbol of lament. There are many indigenous people around the world who grieve over what has been done to their homelands. The powerful usurp the land, animals, water rights or fishing grounds that once sustained the people. Greed, corruption and lack of forethought make some people exiles within their own borders.

Humanity is interconnected with nature. In Romans 8, the apostle Paul tells us that this relationship also carries a future association with God's plan of salvation. Even the natural world strains toward the day of Christ's return. One day creation will be restored.

Sharing the good news of Christ with people is primary. Only God can effect the new creation of the human heart. That new life affects how we treat others and how we care for the environment.

To ponder:

How can we help lessen the toll that environmental ruin takes on people whose voices are unheard?

Cleansing Power

'Only the clean-handed, only the pure-hearted' (Psalm 24:4, MSG).

Today friends send emails or text messages to share news quickly or to arrange to meet on an impulse. During Jesus' ministry, whenever he is in the area, word spreads rapidly too. People with limited resources are thrilled and race to bring their sick loved ones to him. They have hope with Jesus near. From the time the disciples and Jesus anchor at Gennesaret, Galilee, and move onward through the region, people seek him out.

There are always new faces in the crowd. Word must have travelled about the woman who had earlier been healed when she touched Jesus' robe because now others beg to do the same. Jesus honours their faith and heals them as well. But not all who seek out Jesus believe in his mission.

Some of the onlookers are Pharisees and teachers of religious law who come from Jerusalem to investigate and discredit Jesus. They focus on something the disciples fail to do. In verses 3 and 4 Mark gives his non-Jewish readers a brief introduction to what the washing ritual tradition requires. The leaders question Jesus because as the disciples' teacher he is responsible for their actions.

To these detractors to whom tradition and ritual matter most, Jesus poses a threat. They devotedly follow an oral law which was developed through the centuries to amplify and codify the Ten Commandments and the Pentateuch. This is what they mean by the 'tradition of the elders' in verse 5.

Jesus doesn't respond about washing rituals. He knows that the root of their question reveals that their religious authority is tradition, not Scripture, and that for them the nature of defilement is ceremonial, not moral. Their good standing relies on their system. He calls them hypocrites, mere actors on a religious stage rather than genuine believers in God, and quotes Isaiah's prophecy about such hollow lives. He confronts them with their preference for following human cleverness rather than obeying God's commands.

In subsequent verses Jesus clarifies the main issue: what defiles people is what comes out of their hearts. What's needed isn't ceremonial hand-washing, but moral heart-washing. Are you washed?

Can You Hear Me Now?

'People were overwhelmed with amazement. "He has done everything well,"
they said. "He even makes the deaf hear and the mute speak"' (v. 37).

For a short time Jesus instructs the disciples while in non-Jewish regions. He is stressed by recent Jewish leaders' hostility, hometown opposition, Herod's suspicions and zealots' schemes. He heads northwest out of Galilee. Perhaps the forty-mile hike allows for some mental relief from the taxing ministry and some time for Jesus and the disciples to get in step with each other.

But even when he's in Phoenicia trying to stay in an undisclosed location, people discover he's there. First on the scene is a Greek woman appealing to him to heal her little girl who is at home. After what seems friendly banter, Jesus tells her to go home, the demonic affliction has left her daughter. It is so.

The disciples are learning to remove barriers. When Jesus responded to the Jewish leaders, he challenged distinctions between clean and unclean foods. His actions in Phoenicia challenge the notion of distinguishing people groups as clean and unclean. What his followers learn from Jesus about the nature of the kingdom of God continues to astound them.

When they leave Tyre they continue north for twenty-five miles to Sidon before they start the long return trek south. Mark doesn't explain the detour. No doubt Jesus takes time to try to crystallise the disciples' understanding of his mission and to enjoy their fellowship before the weight of his final days.

When they arrive in the vicinity of the Sea of Galilee, they don't head to Capernaum, but east of the lake in yet another predominantly Gentile region, Decapolis, where Jesus healed the demon-possessed man. The man's witness may have inspired those who now flock to Jesus for help.

People bring a deaf man for Jesus' healing touch. Thoughtfully, Jesus takes him aside and motions to him what he intends to do. He looks toward heaven, heaves a deep sigh and gives the command. Even the word he uses for 'be opened' may have been one the man could easily lip-read. *Immediately* Isaiah's prophecy is fulfilled as the Messiah restores hearing, speech and more (Isaiah 35:5, 6). Christ longs to open our hearts to hear him better.

Long-expected Jesus

'He said to them, "Do you still not understand?"' (v. 21)

A crowd have been with Jesus for three days, so have perhaps exhausted what provisions they brought. He wants to be sure they have nourishment before they head for home.

Earlier Jesus fed more than five thousand hungry seekers who'd come to hear him near the north shore of the lake. This time the disciples don't talk about how much it will cost, only how little is available in such a remote area. Once again with limited resources of bread and fish Jesus feeds more than four thousand who gather to hear him in Decapolis. This time there are seven large baskets of leftovers. Christ cares about all our needs and provides abundantly.

Jesus sees the people off, then he and his disciples embark for the other side of the lake. Dalmanutha is not far from Herod's palace. Mark only mentions this one incident there, a disconcerting encounter Jesus has with the contentious Pharisees. The group is back on the boat heading for Bethsaida, their one-time intended retreat spot that had turned into a picnic site for more than five thousand.

Jesus warns about the yeast of the Pharisees and of Herod. The disciples hear 'yeast' and think 'bread'. They don't catch Jesus' metaphor for the corrupting influences of the legalists and the political. Even after seeing Jesus' recent miraculous provision of food for the thousands, the disciples think they're being reprimanded for bringing only one loaf of bread.

Jesus has recently restored a deaf man's hearing and would soon restore a blind man's sight. Yet his disciples act as if they're deaf and blind to things of the kingdom and to God's presence. Do they sense his allusion to the Old Testament prophets' reproof when he reproaches: 'Do you have eyes but fail to see, and ears but fail to hear' (v. 18)?

The disciples are the same people he has told on more than one occasion that he is showing them things that others with less interest in the kingdom can't see or understand and have to be given by parable only. The disciples still aren't sure about who Jesus really is. They haven't seized their opportunity to believe what his words and his works demonstrate.

Do we believe who the long-expected Jesus is and that he's with us?

Once More

'Once more Jesus put his hands on the man's eyes. Then his eyes were opened, his sight was restored, and he saw everything clearly' (v. 25).

Mark's Gospel is the only one to tell about Jesus healing the deaf man in the Decapolis region and the only one to record Jesus' two-step healing of a blind man near Bethsaida. Apparently his source (Peter) finds Jesus' encounters with these individuals significant.

Once again people bring the one in need to Jesus. Once again they implore him to touch the man. Perhaps they attribute Jesus' healing power to something rare in the Master's body with which contact has to be made. Again Jesus shows consideration for the individual as he takes the person in need aside, this time by the hand.

Again Jesus uses his saliva in the healing process, an action people of that day understand as curative. The man can see, but only partially – as if he has cataracts. His simile – men as walking trees – perhaps makes us think of the tree people of Narnia.

We wonder if this occasion's rare two-step process of healing is for the disciples' benefit. Since sight was used in their day as a metaphor for insight, the man's partial sight may remind them of what Jesus said in the boat. At present they have poor spiritual vision. Jesus touches the man's eyes and his sight is fully restored. There is hope for the disciples. Perhaps soon they too will see clearly.

As he has done a number of times when it is necessary to safeguard his wider mission, Jesus asks the one he's helped not to broadcast what happened. He sends him home, but expressly he's not to go via the village. This may be for the newly sighted man's sake as well. He needs time to adjust and reflect before answering everyone's questions. His story eventually is told and retold.

Besides the miracle, what did Peter see in this event that made him ensure Mark would record it? He values people who bring others to Jesus. His brother brought him (John 1:41). He notices the considerate way Jesus deals with people's real needs. He recognises how persistent and skilful Jesus is in using every opportunity to unlock kingdom truth even to sometimes bumbling followers. He sees that Jesus seeks an authentic relationship with each individual.

Not Parenthetical, Pivotal

'Then he called the crowd to him along with his disciples and said:
"If anyone would come after me, he must deny himself and take up
his cross and follow me" ' (v. 34).

With the close of Mark 8 we come to the end of another major section of Mark's Gospel. Two previous sections finished with statements of rejection. In chapter 3 the Pharisees and Herodians began to plot to destroy Jesus. In chapter 6 the lack of faith of his hometown neighbours thwarted Jesus from any mighty work. This section concludes very differently, with Peter's acknowledgment of the Christ.

Jesus and the disciples walk toward Mount Hermon. Perhaps they follow the Jordan River north to Caesarea Philippi, located near its source. Along the way Jesus asks who the disciples have heard people say he is. It may seem to be a parenthetical conversation. The disciples are free with their replies, which probably reflect some of their own thoughts.

Opposition is mounting. Things would soon come to a head for Jesus. Whatever the disciples believed, Jesus was moving toward the cross. Their recognition of him as Messiah was crucial. So Jesus dares to ask them who they think he is. Previously the disciples have heard demons identify him, but few others. Ever-ready Peter answers for all of them, 'You are the Christ', the Messiah (v. 29). Finally, one of his own gets it right.

The Jews had developed expectations for their Messiah. He would be from the Davidic line and arrive when chaos threatened to take over. An 'Elijah' would help prepare his way and announce him. Nations would band together to oppose him, but he would take vengeance on them. Jerusalem would be restored and Jews would stream back to the golden city to a new era of peace.

Peter's momentous declaration will steady them in a storm greater than any the disciples have faced at sea. It is a starting point, but Jesus needs to re-educate them about the true nature of the Messiah. He speaks plainly about his death. Peter's protest angers him.

A suffering Saviour has implications for his followers. They aren't ready to proclaim him until they can personally embrace the cost of the cross. That paradox, placed central in Mark's Gospel, is the pivotal matter for our lives as well.

Notes

1. *Bringing Scripture Alive!, vol. 2, Mark My Word*, with DVD (ISBN 978-0-89216-114-0). © 2008, The Salvation Army, USA Eastern Territory, West Nyack, New York, USA.

2. Lieut-Colonel Marlene Chase, in *Our God Comes*, © 2000, Crest Books, The Salvation Army, Alexandria, Virginia, USA.

3. H. W. Fowler, *Modern English Usage*, Clarendon Press, Oxford, 1958.

4. Babbie Mason, *With All My Heart* © Word Music (song permanently out of print).

5. Keith Banks, *The Greatest Adventure A Spiritual Journey in Poetry and Song with Keith and Pauline Banks* © 2008 Radiovision Networks, Largs, Scotland.

6. *Commentaire au Cantique des Cantiques de Salomon* (Commentary on Solomon's Song of Songs), 1688.

7. Watchman Nee, *The Song of Songs*, © 1965, Christian Literature Crusade, Pennsylvania, USA.

8. Hannah Hurnard, *Mountains of Spices*, Tyndale House, Illinois, 1983.

9. Watchman Nee, *The Song of Songs*, © 1965, Christian Literature Crusade, Pennsylvania, USA.

10. W. Phillip Keller, *Walking With God*, Kregal Publications, Grand Rapids, Michigan, USA, 1998.

11. *Young People's Songs*, The Salvation Army, 1951, Chicago, USA.

12. William Barclay, *The Daily Study Bible Series: The Letters to the Corinthians* (St Andrew Press, Edinburgh, 1954, revised and updated by St Andrew Press, 1975).

13. Michel Quoist, *Prayers of Life*, Gill & Macmillan Ltd, Dublin, Ireland, 1965.

14. Graham Kendrick © 1988, Make Way Music.

15. Richard A. Swenson, MD, *Restoring Emotional, Physical, Financial, and Time Reserves to Overloaded Lives*, NavPress, 2004.

16. Philip Yancey, *Reaching for the Invisible God*, © 2000, The Zondervan Corporation, Grand Rapids, Michigan, USA.

17. Quoted by Philip Yancey in *Reaching for the Invisible God*, © 2000, The Zondervan Corporation, Grand Rapids, Michigan, USA.

18. *Adult Faith Connections Bible Study Guide*, © 2008, WordAction Publishing Company, Kansas City, Missouri, USA.

19. From Luci Shaw's book of poems, *The Sighting* (Wheaton Literary Series), Shaw Books, Wheaton, Illinois, USA, 2000.

20. From 'Upon this Rock' by Gloria Gaither and Dony McGuire, © 1986 by Gaither Music Company.

Index

Subscribe...

Words of Life is published three times a year:
January–April, May–August and September–December

Four easy ways to subscribe

- By post – simply complete and return the subscription form below
- By phone – +44 (0)1933 445 445
- By email – mail_order@sp-s.co.uk
- Or visit your local Christian bookshop

SUBSCRIPTION FORM

Name (Miss, Mrs, Ms, Mr)...

Address ....

....

.... Postcode ....

Tel. No..

Email* ....

Annual Subscription Rates

UK **£10.50**   *Non-UK* £10.50 + £3.90 P&P = **£14.40**

Please send me .... copy/copies of the next three issues of *Words of Life* commencing with **May 2010**

Total: £ .... I enclose payment by cheque ☐

Please make cheques payable to *The Salvation Army*

Please debit my Access/Mastercard/Visa/American Express/Switch card

Card No. ☐☐☐☐ ☐☐☐☐ ☐☐☐☐ ☐☐☐☐   Expiry date: ___ /___

Security No. ☐☐☐ Issue number (Switch only) _____

Cardholder's signature: .... Date: ....

Please send this form and any cheques to: The Mail Order Department, Salvationist Publishing and Supplies, 66–78 Denington Road, Denington Industrial Estate, Wellingborough, Northamptonshire NN8 2QH, UK

☐ *We would like to keep in touch with you by placing you on our mailing list. If you would prefer not to receive correspondence from us, please tick this box. The Salvation Army does not sell or lease its mailing lists.